A Tribute to George Helm & Kimo Mitchell

Edited By Rodney Morales

Bamboo Ridge Press
1984

This is a special issue of *Bamboo Ridge, The Hawaii Writers' Quarterly,* No. 22, Spring 1984.

Library of Congress Catalog Number 84-70273
ISBN 0-910043-08-6
ISSN 0733-0308

Published by Bamboo Ridge Press
Cover: Steve Shrader
Typesetting: Creative Impressions
Production: Sun, an educational communications co.
Printing: Pioneer Printers

Aloha 'Aina," by the Protect Kahoolawe Ohana was previously published in *Na Mana'o Aloha o Kaho'olawe.* Reprinted by permission.

"Aloha 'Aina," by Kalani Meinecke, was originally published in the liner notes to Aunty Edith Kanakaole's album, *Hi'ipoi I Ka 'Aina.* Reprinted with permission of Hula Records.

"Ballad of George Helm" and "Molokai Sweet Home" printed with permission of Malani Bilyeu.

"Death At Sea" was originally published in *Mana, a South Pacific Journal of Language and Literature* (Vol. 6, No. 1, 1981). Reprinted with permission of Richard Hamasaki and Mark Hamasaki.

"E Mau" (Let's Strive) printed with permission of Alvin K. Isaacs, Sr.

George Helm photo on p. 74 printed with permission of the *Honolulu Advertiser.*

"George Helm," by 'Ilima Pi'ianai'a, was originally published in *Hawaii Observer,* No. 102, April 5, 1977. Reprinted with permission of author.

"George Helm—Aloha Week 1980" was originally published in *Bamboo Ridge, The Hawaii Writers' Quarterly.* Reprinted with permission of Eric Chock.

"Hawaiian Soul." Reprinted with permission of Starnight Records.

"Huaka'i" was previously published in *The Hawaiian News.* Reprinted with permission of Joseph P. Balaz.

Liner Notes for *Islands* printed with permission of Don Chapman and the *Honolulu Advertiser.*

Kahoolawe Chants, Legends, Poems, Stories by Children of Maui was previously published in *Seaweeds and Constructions* (No. 5, 1978). Reprinted with permission of Wayne K. Westlake.

Kimo Mitchell photo on p. 90 printed with permission of the *Honolulu Star-Bulletin.*

"Mele o Kahoolawe" (Song of Kahoolawe) printed with permission of Harry K. Mitchell, Sr.

"Moe'uhane" was previously published in *The Hawaiian News* and *Kaala.* Reprinted with permission of Joseph P. Balaz.

"Molokai Miracle." Reprinted with permission of Fortunato Teho and the *Honolulu Advertiser.*

"Seven Pools." Printed with permission of Harry K. Mitchell, Sr.

"Where Does It All Lead To." Printed with permission of author.

Bamboo Ridge Press, P.O. Box 61781, Honolulu, HI 96839-1781

10 9 8 7 6 5 4 94 95 96

This tribute is dedicated to the *keiki o ka'aina,* whose strength and dignity are nurtured by the sacrifices made by George Helm and Kimo Mitchell. This tribute is especially dedicated to the Helm and Mitchell *mo'opuna,* whose receptive eyes, easy-going laughter, and unfailing generosity are gentle reminders that through them their uncles live on.

Contents

Introduction	6	RODNEY MORALES
George Helm—The Voice and Soul	10	RODNEY MORALES
Molokai Miracle	34	FORTUNATO TEHO
Poem	37	RUTH NAKAMURA
E Mau (Let's Strive)	38	ALVIN K. ISAACS, SR.
Hawaiian Soul	41	JON OSORIO and RANDY BORDEN
Liner Notes for *Islands*	42	DON CHAPMAN
Molokai Sweet Home	43	MALANI BILYEU
Ballad of George Helm	44	MALANI BILYEU
Story	45	CALVIN TASAKA
George Helm	47	ʻILIMA PIʻIANAIʻA
Untitled (Drawing and Poem)	50	IMAIKALANI KALAHELE
Poem	52	LESTER NAKAMOTO
Poem	53	JOY BLAKESLEE
Poem	53	ELLEN ENOKI
Personal Statement	55	GEORGE HELM
Legend	56	LEHUA HOUGH
Poem for George Helm—Aloha Week 1980	57	ERIC CHOCK
PKO Testimony in Support of H.B. 1129	60	GEORGE HELM and LORETTA RITTE
Telegram to President Carter	62	GEORGE HELM, FRANCIS KAUHANE, CHARLES WARRINGTON
Poem	64	JILL HARWOOD
Letter to President Carter	65	GEORGE HELM, FRANCIS KAUHANE
Poem	67	TRACY LANI DELATORI
Speech to the State House	69	GEORGE HELM
Diary Entry—Fourth Occupation of Kahoolawe	72	GEORGE HELM
George Helm—A True Hawaiian	73	WALTER RITTE, JR.

Kimo Mitchell—A Life	76	RODNEY MORALES
Seven Pools	85	JAMES KIMO MITCHELL and HARRY K. MITCHELL
Mele o Kahoolawe (Song of Kahoolawe)	86	HARRY KUNIHI MITCHELL
Poem	88	KEITH KARLO
Poem	88	ANN KAWABATA
Poem	88	ROBIN BODINUS
Story	89	ELMO SAVELLA
Story	89	LORI ZIMMERMAN
Remembering Kimo	90	KAULUA
Moe'uhane	91	JOSEPH P. BALAZ
Aloha 'Aina	92	KALANI MEINECKE
Aloha 'Aina	93	PROTECT KAHOOLAWE OHANA
Story	94	JACKIE MAILE KAANANA
Poem	94	ARIANNA ALTFELD
Legend	95	ANDY PELE
Chant	95	SAMUEL WAIOHU
Map 1—The Search	96	
Map 2—Maui/Kahoolawe	98	
Map 3—Kahoolawe	99	
Malamalama	100	
Death At Sea	101	RICHARD HAMASAKI, MARK HAMASAKI
Poem	102	TAMMY LABORTE
Poem	102	ALLEN DARISAY
Where Does It All Lead To	103	KIHEI
In The Spirit of George and Kimo	105	EMMETT ALULI
Huaka'i	110	JOSEPH P. BALAZ
Kahoolawe Remembers	111	WAYNE MUROMOTO
Notes on Contributors	112	

Introduction

Rodney Morales

Around March 6 or 7, 1977, two young men disappeared off the waters of Kahoolawe. George Helm, 26, a musician and president of the Protect Kahoolawe Ohana, and Kimo Mitchell, 25, a commercial fisherman and National Park Service Ranger from Keanae, were never seen or heard from again. Now—seven years later at this writing—though considered *legally* dead, there is no doubt that George and Kimo are alive in spirit. They still move the hearts and stir the minds of people old and young. Hopefully, the pages that follow help to explain why they do.

Those who contributed to this book were touched in some way by George and Kimo. Some knew them personally; others did not. All, though, were touched with the impulse to create, an impulse, it seems, to *ho'okupu* (to give, to cause to grow) "the good bruddahs" who talked and lived *aloha 'aina* (love for the land; giving in return to what gives you life).

Ho'iHo'i Hou (giving back, returning, restoring, restitution) came into significant use in the 1890s. After the overthrow of Liliuokalani in 1893, *Ho'iHo'i Hou* was a cry uttered by Royalists who wanted their beloved queen back on the throne and the Hawaiian monarchy restored. A similar term, *Ho'iHo'i Ea,* or restoration of sovereignty, was used in 1843, when Admiral Richard Thomas—the "highest representative of Her Majesty Queen Victoria"—returned the throne to Hawaiian hands six months after Captain George Paulet had—without orders—claimed the throne for England in 1842. Admiral Thomas interceded on behalf of Kamehameha III and declared him the legitimate king. King Kamehameha III, when given back his sovereignty, stated *Ua mau ke ea o ka aina i ka pono,* the life of the land is perpetuated in righteousness—now Hawaii's state motto.

George Helm and Kimo Mitchell *died* trying to *live* our state motto. Their concern to perpetuate the righteousness of *ka aina* led to their untimely deaths.

This tribute is one attempt to restore dignity to their lives, partly because labels attributed to Helm and Mitchell—like "Hawaiian activist"—simply do not suffice; partly to reciprocate for what they have given to us all—the spirit of *aloha 'aina,* the spirit of *'ohana.* And because they are with us *in spirit,* they are whom we turn to for *inspiration,* and in that sense they are *always* returning.

Ho'iHo'i Hou is a warm mahalo to George Helm and Kimo Mitchell.

Mahalo also to: the Helm and Mitchell families, without whose support and encouragement this tribute wouldn't have, couldn't have been done; Richard Hamasaki and Eric Chock, co-inspiritors; Darrell Lum, Ann Morales, and Lizabeth Ball, for editorial assistance, mapping, and prodding; Dr. Emmett Aluli and Mark Matsunaga, facilitators; and Wayne Kaumualii Westlake, whose Kahoolawe Children's Poems are flung like jewels throughout the pages, like islands in the sea.

Mahalo to all who contributed, in all ways.

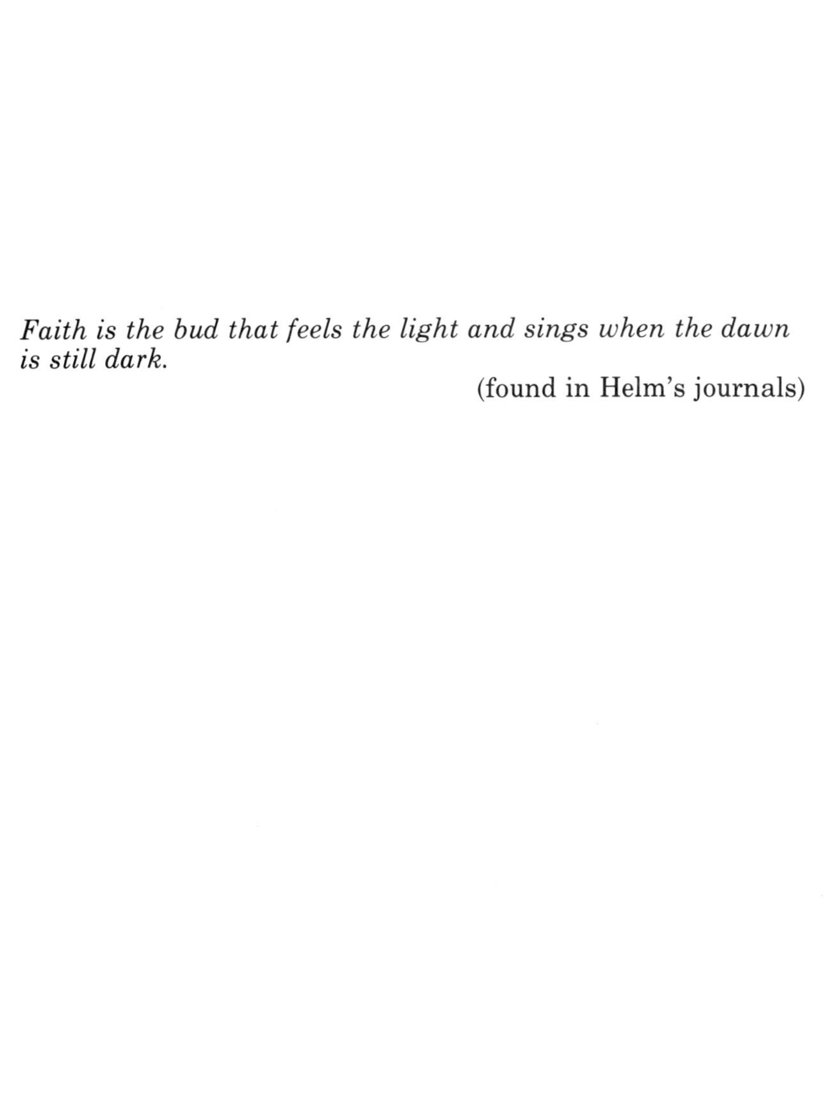

Faith is the bud that feels the light and sings when the dawn is still dark.

(found in Helm's journals)

10 George Helm—The Voice and Soul

Rodney Morales

George Jarrett Helm, Jr., was born on March 23, 1950, at the Hawaiian homestead of Kalamaula on the island of Molokai. He was the fifth of seven children, the middle boy among five. There was little in his early years to differentiate George from many other Hawaiian kids. Along with his brothers and sisters he spent many hours helping out on the family farm, where their father grew prize cantaloupes and the family raised ducks, pigs, rabbits, and chickens. And like most Hawaiian kids, he spent hours at the beach—cooling off in the water from the hot Hawaiian sun, fishing for mullet, Samoan crab, and *'opae,* or chasing crabs on the rocks for after school snacks as if there never need be a *McDonald's.*

When they were not farming, fishing, or going to school, the Helm kids were active in sports. Their father, George Helm, Sr.—an intense man of Hawaiian-Portuguese-German-English-Welsh ancestry—taught his kids—the boys especially—the rudiments of basketball and baseball. Older brothers Larry and Gregory also helped to coach and guide George, Zachary and Adolph, the three youngest, in this respect.

But George, Sr., provided George, or Jarry-boy as he was called then, with something more. He placed an ukulele and then a guitar in his son's hands, taught him chords, and passed on to George, Jr., his love for Hawaiian music. Melanie Koko Helm, George's mother, a full-blooded Hawaiian, recalls that three-year-old Jarry-boy used to take his ukulele to bed with him and sleep with it as if it were a teddy bear.

Essentially, George grew up in a rural farm setting and absorbed the cultural values that nurtured what he would years later refer to as "Hawaiian conscience," or "Hawaiian soul." Though he was inclined to moments of introspection, George could also be very outgoing. Like his siblings, he had a warm personality and a keen sense of humor. He could be as funny as he could be serious. He embraced extremes.

He was also hard-headed. George had a mean temper, family members recall, and he usually showed it by punching

Alexis Higdon

some inanimate object, usually a wall. His father provided him with a safety valve by instructing him to say five "Hail Marys" whenever he got worked up about something. This suggestion helped.

Obviously, the Helms were a Catholic family. George's mother, who had been born in Hana and later raised in Honolulu at a convent school, brought up her children in the Church. She was especially proud when George was offered an athletic scholarship to St. Louis High School in Honolulu. Before that he had attended Holomua and Kaunakakai elementary schools, Molokai Intermediate School, and Molokai High School.

So in 1965, at the age of fifteen, Jarry-boy, an innocent in the ways of the world, set out for the big city. What he experienced in Honolulu can only be described as cultural shock.

He was laughed at because of his homemade clothes, *puka* T-shirts, socks that didn't match. He was country, all right. The nickname Jarry-boy gave way to "Molokai." Furthermore, his initial loneliness in the city was magnified by his having to move from one residence to another. First he lived with his uncle Elias Koko, then with his older sister Stephanie, then with the family of high school friend Gary Loo. Later he moved in with sister Georgia-Mae.

Though the nickname "Molokai" may have been used teasingly at first, later on it was used with respect. Molokai is known as the friendly island and George's warmth and sense of humor won him a lot of friends.

George had won the scholarship for baseball, but basketball became his favorite sport. He played on the St. Louis basketball team that won the state championship and went undefeated during his two years there. He played as a reserve, not a starter. In any other year, some say, he would have been a star, but he played for St. Louis when they had their legendary starting five: Jim Nicholson, Howie Dunnam, Larry Frank, Glenn Hookano, and Donald Mahi.

When the team was not winning games they were a notorious bunch of clowns, and George was their clown prince. (He

George Helm in 1973 at the Waikiki Shell.

Ed Greevy

was once rushed to St. Francis Hospital in pain because of a severe hemorrhoidal condition. When friends came to the hospital to see him, he said, "Oh. Baby boy.") George kept their spirits up with his antics—and his cheers. Once, coach Walter Wong decided to throw George off the team because he was always fooling around and not taking practice seriously enough. After hearing the news, George cried and angrily pounded the gym lockers with his fists. The other players backed George up. They told Coach Wong that they needed him, that he was the heart of the team. After some deliberation, Wong decided to keep him on.

Though George lacked size—he was five foot eight—his determination more than made up for it. Once, during a casual game at Manoa Gym, George kept trying to play with a sprained ankle, hobbling up and down the basketball court till he could no longer take the pain. He would sit down for a while then go back into the game, rest when the pain was unbearable, go back in again, and so on until the other players had to tell him to quit. He was *intense.*

The same determination George showed in sports was paralleled in the field of music. He joined the student Glee Club directed by John Lake, who later introduced George to his cousin Kahauanu Lake, a noted teacher and performer of Hawaiian chants and music. Together the Lakes redirected George's musical tastes from rock and roll to Hawaiian. Soon George was performing as a dancer for Kahauanu Lake's show at the Kaimana Hotel. He also spent long hours after school at Kahauanu Lake's home, studying music (and cleaning the yard to earn extra cash). Lake became George's musical mentor; he taught him how to sing parts and develop a fine falsetto. (His relatives used to call him "da frog" when he tried to sing. No more.) And as a guitarist, George learned to play—with his "Molokai stroke"—everything from flamenco to slack key. Friends say: *Music. That was his magic.*

Kahauanu Lake taught George the one lesson that stayed with him till the end. Lake stressed the importance of fully understanding and rightfully representing Hawaiian culture, and had his students translate and learn the background of the songs and chants they performed. George would later be known for his meticulousness, for his thorough probing into all aspects of the Hawaiian experience. "Do your homework," George would say repeatedly to friends and acquaintances. Implicit in his way of stating this was that he had done his.

After graduating from St. Louis, George did a six-week summer stint in Japan, performing Hawaiian music with a teenage troupe. Then it was on to college. George attended Brigham Young University-Hawaii, Leeward Community College, and the University of Hawaii-Manoa. After "floundering around," he dropped out of college in 1972, just short of graduation, and parlayed his musical talent and his Molokai charm into getting a job as a sales representative for Hawaiian Airlines. Later, he traveled throughout the world as a good-will ambassador for the airlines and for the tourist industry. His one noted coup, so to speak, took place in Mexico City, where he convinced the representatives of the forty-five-thousand-member Lions Club to hold their next convention on the shores of Waikiki. George Helm, in the eyes of the business world, was on his way.

From 1972 through 1974, while living most of the time with sister Georgia-Mae, George behaved very much like "someone on his way." He took to wearing expensive clothes. Made sure his socks always matched. His hair was always neatly combed back. And for a brief period he sported a goatee and a trim mustache. Georgia-Mae says he brought a lot of girls home, usually dancers from the Hawaiian shows he frequented, but had a decided preference for the intelligent ones. He continued to travel a lot, all over the mainland and to the Orient. He grew distant from his family.

But the Western style of success did not fit this part-Hawaiian kid from Molokai. A significant change came over him after a trip to New York. In the clutter and grime, the harsh competitiveness, the alienation of big city life he saw Honolulu's and perhaps Hawaii's future, a future he could not

"Big business has turned the 'spirit of aloha' into a commodity."

(All quotations that are uncredited are those of George Helm.)

live comfortably with. He said that the asphalt was "suffocating." George quit his airlines job and began to pursue his musical career—not for the money, but to stay true to things that mattered most to him. Later he would say, "I divorced myself from the tourist industry to do Hawaiian music. It's in my blood."

His growing knowledge of Hawaiian music led him to places uncharted by most Hawaiians his age. He found in many of the songs he was singing—not overly commercial *hapa haole* ones but more authentic ones based on Hawaiian experiences—stories of a deeply saddened yet still proud people. Songs like Alvin Isaacs' "E Mau" touched him with their mournful yet strong spirit. Alvin Isaacs, patriarch of the talented Isaacs family, became an inspiration to him. So did Richard Kauhi, an artist who explored "progressive Hawaiian" music, and Andy Cummings, who had performed with George for Hawaiian Airlines and taught him to appreciate hapa-haole songs like "Dancing Under the Stars" and "Waikiki."

George's reputation as a singer/musician grew quickly. He signed a contract with Holiday Inn and began performing, first alone, then with partner Homer Hu, at the Windjammer Room in the 6-9 dinner slot. Later they were joined by Wayne Reis and performed as Kekumu (The Source) at the Imperial Lounge and at Castagnola's Lobster House. Wayne Harada, the *Honolulu Advertiser* reviewer, wrote with glowing praise of this talented group who sounded "remarkably like the Kahauanu Lake Trio." By then George was very much part of the entertainment scene. To speak generally, he knew all the other entertainers. George ran around with the younger ones, like members of the group Kalapana, but sometimes hung around venerable ones like Genoa Keawe and Edith Kanaka'ole. He grew especially close to the latter. When he needed his spirits lifted, he often flew over to Hilo, on the Big Island, and shared his *mana'o* (feelings, thoughts) and music with Auntie Edith, a multi-talented woman who, with only a sixth-grade education, still was sufficiently skilled in

Photo courtesy of the PKO

Helm with Aunty Edith and Wayne Reis.

Hawaiian language, chants, and songs to be given a teaching position at the University of Hawaii's Hilo campus. (Once, to celebrate her birthday, George flew over to Hilo to surprise her with a special performance of all her favorite songs.)

One event that brought George closer to his family, if only temporarily, was his father's hospitalization (for unspecified reasons) on Oahu. George wrote to everyone in his family: to Larry in Seattle, to Zachary in Los Angeles, to the others on Molokai, urging them to write to their father. "He needs our help," he told them. (George Helm, Sr., had been a highly praised farmer (*See* "Molokai Miracle") at one time, but had been victimized by a series of mishaps. One year a flood ruined his crops because the Hawaiian Homes Commission was negligent in clearing some drainage ditches. In another year, his crops were poisoned in a pesticide accident when a utility company sprayed the roadside areas. George would relate later how these misfortunes broke his father's spirit and discouraged him in his farming efforts.) Ironically, while George was very concerned about his father's getting well, the senior George Helm was busy outfoxing doctors and nurses and reportedly snuck out of the hospital more than once.

George visited his father regularly, usually bringing his guitar. (His father loved to hear him sing.) It got to be that when George arrived with his guitar, other patients would be sitting there, waiting to hear the boy with the soothing voice.

In 1975, the organization Hui Alaloa (Group of the Long Trails), was formed on the island of Molokai. Original members included Walter Ritte, Jr., a former Kamehameha and University of Hawaii basketball star; Dr. Emmett Aluli, Oahu born, a Marquette University and University of Hawaii medical school graduate who was an *extern* practicing rural medicine on Molokai; and Adolph Helm, George's farmer-fisherman brother, who had done a stint with the Navy. Hui Alaloa organized to gain access to the mountains and beaches that had for years been closed off to the general public.

One day that year, Adolph introduced George, who was visiting from Honolulu, to Ritte and Aluli. They discovered in George the kind of talent and energy they sorely needed. He could write precisely and with lucidity. Also, his knowledge of Hawaiiana put the others to shame. And speaking of shame, no one dared to pass out leaflets in the town of Kaunakakai. ("Shame. We know everybody" was the usual excuse) until George himself grabbed a batch and canvassed the town, talking at length to anyone who had the time, making his case against the big landowners with conviction and a good assessment of the facts. He was the first to openly defy the island's largest landowner, Molokai Ranch. After that, everyone got braver. Marches were organized which led to the opening of two rights-of-way to the beaches.

Back in Honolulu, George carried on his work for Hui Alaloa. When not performing his music he carried on the group's research into land titles, access rights, and read for hours at a time. He wrote everything down, almost obsessively. Notes to himself, usually in journals, occasionally on napkins; diary-like recordings of the day's or previous day's events; drafts of personal letters or letters written on behalf of Hui Alaloa (often with the opening paragraph written over and over until he was satisfied that he got it right); comments on his relationships with others; quotes from his readings....As his social concerns grew, his interest in metaphysics grew correspondingly. Although George expressed that he wasn't well read, the fact that he often quoted Carl S. Jung and Friedrich Nietzsche, and, to a lesser extent, Somerset Maugham, Rainer Maria Rilke, Theodore Roszak, and Andre Gide suggests otherwise and reveals the range of his readings. He seemed to be well versed in religion, mythology, philosophy, and psychology. In Hui Alaloa and in the struggles that were to follow, he found *practical* uses for his *abstract* ideas.

1976 was a turbulent year for George Helm. During the last fourteen months of his life—from January 1976 to March 1977—he was surrounded by and caught up in events that are potentially as significant to Hawaiians as Captain James Cook's arrival and the 1893 overthrow of the Hawaiian monarchy. On the other hand, the potential impact may never be realized and may someday fizzle out completely like so many fireworks displays.

But in 1976, the year of America's bicentennial, everything that had gone wrong, and right, in Hawaii had come to a head. And at the center of the swirl of events—stood George Helm.

It started like this: On January 3, 1976, nine people landed on the "target island" of Kahoolawe. (Kahoolawe, situated off the southern coast of Maui and the smallest of the eight major islands in the Hawaiian chain, had been used for bombing practice by the United States Navy since 1941. The island and its surrounding waters were off limits to everyone but the U.S. military. Fishermen have long complained that they weren't able to fish in its pristine waters.) The nine included Helm, Ritte, and Aluli of Hui Alaloa, who had been asked to go along by Charles Maxwell, the organizer of the landing, because of their success on Molokai. Also in on the landing were Ellen Miles, Karla Villalba, Kimo Aluli, Ian Lind, and members of the Hawaiian Coalition for Native Claims (HCNC) Gail Prejean and Stephen Morse. The landing was not well planned nor well thought out. One day they were talking about it. The next they were there.

All except Ritte and Aluli—who had gone into the *kiawe* thicket to relieve themselves—were caught by the Coast Guard minutes after the landing. Ritte and Aluli lay low and ended up spending two days on the island before giving themselves up. They underwent what they described as a religious experience. Aluli talked of feeling "like we were just coming out of the ocean and walking on new lands." Ritte said that he could not understand why but he cried for hours during his first night there. It was a turning point in both their lives, to say the least. And in the lives of many individuals, including George Helm.

Helm and others spoke of how they had thought the island

> "What greater grief than the loss of one's native land."
> Euripides

was a barren rock. They were surprised by its beauty, and angered by its being misused. Helm saw his role as that of organizer, getting people behind the issue of Kahoolawe. Protests were aimed at the military. "Stop the bombing" became a common cry. Helm stated to a *Hawaii Observer* reporter that "It was incredible to watch the thing grow... we were touched by some force that pushed us into commitment." Thus, at age 25, Helm became the prime mover, the leader, of the Protect Kahoolawe Association (later the Protect Kahoolawa Ohana—PKO). He travelled from island to island—primarily where Hawaiians were clustered: homestead lands, places like Hana, Maui; Keaukaha on the Big Island—going from house to house, attending community gatherings, not only to talk about Kahoolawe (which he said was the symbol of the many wrongs afflicting Hawaiians as well as the catalyst for solving them) but also to find out the problems and issues of each area.

In every area that he visited, he found the common problems of loss of hunting and fishing rights, loss of land through adverse possession, loss of water rights, and the lack of good land to farm or, worse, no land at all. Though all Hawaiians were entitled to homestead lands, many were kept on waiting lists for decades, waiting to receive the lands that were rightfully theirs. Much of the homestead land was leased to non-Hawaiians. (Hawaiian Homes commissioners justify this seeming misallocation by asserting that such leases brought in the revenue needed to develop housing units on homestead land.)

Absence from the land seemed to be the common thread linking many of the problems that Hawaiians had. Kahoolawe was an extreme example of this. The catch phrase for a solution to these problems became "aloha 'aina." *Aloha 'aina,* simply put, means love for the land. But its meaning goes deeper than that. It is the practical yet much ignored notion that you take care of the land because it takes care of you. (The *re-emergence* of this term takes on an added, mystical dimension. Helm said that during the initial landing on Kahoolawe, he and others began saying "aloha 'aina"—out of the blue. They had no knowledge of the implications of the

"We should not pretend to understand the world only by the intellect; we apprehend it just as much by feeling. Therefore the judgment of the intellect is, at best, only the half of truth, and must, if it be honest, also come to an understanding of its inadequacy."

Carl Gustav Jung

phrase, nor its historical significance. Later, while doing some research, Helm discovered that "aloha 'aina" was a commonly used term around the time of Queen Liliuokalani's overthrow in 1893. There was a newspaper, *Ke Aloha 'Aina,* started by Judge Joseph Nawahi, and "aloha 'aina" was the password the night that Royalists, counter-revolutionaries loyal to the queen, attempted but failed to restore the Hawaiian monarchy.)

In the meantime, there had been more landings. On Monday, January 14, 1976, Aluli and Ritte again went to Kahoolawe, along with Ritte's wife Loretta and his sister Scarlet. Aluli left two days later—picked up by KGMB TV reporter Bambi Weil, who had just "happened by" on a helicopter—because of his commitments to emergency patients at Queen's Medical Center. The Rittes were all picked up and arrested that Saturday. Aluli and Walter Ritte faced criminal charges because it was their second arrest for trespassing.

At this point, the Protect Kahoolawe Association decided to ask the Navy's permission to go to the island to perform religious ceremonies, and Helm wrote a letter expressing the sincerity of the request. He stated that the ceremonies were necessary to cleanse the island of its evil and to symbolically accept the responsibility of caring for it. This change in strategy paid off, for on February 13, 1976, sixty-five people were allowed by the Navy to land on Kahoolawe and participate in *ho'okupu* (gift-giving) and *mohai aloha* (love offering) ceremonies.

(Also important to note is that while Ritte won his court case on a technicality, Aluli challenged the courts on the grounds of religious freedom. The lawyers, mostly young, idealistic, and Hawaii born, sought out Helm's assistance in defining what exactly is Hawaiian religion. Largely because of Helm's hardnosed research, Aluli also won his case. Helm took the victory to heart; it was an important step toward perpetuation (as opposed to preservation, like in museums) of the Hawaiian culture.)

Helm's journals that year reveal a strong desire to not

Helm with his mother, Melanie "Aunty Mae" Helm, rt., before Hui Alaloa march. Woman in center is Barbara Hanchett.

Photo courtesy of the PKO

just know the Hawaiian culture, but to live it. On one page he writes as the spokesperson for the PKA, on another page he waxes poetic on the beauty of Molokai as seen from an airplane. He struggles with words to describe the lush green valleys and the waterfalls along Molokai's northern coastline. Then he gets philosophical. Phrases like "the beast in man," "the wounded soul of our people," begin to pop up every now and then. He quotes Nietzsche: "Socrates was responsible for rationalism and the bringing about of the theoretical man—Socrates destroyed the instinctive power of man, who became the enemy of myth and tragedy." He also writes, "Jung studied mythology and its relation to the instinctual part of man's personality." In Nietzsche and Jung Helm found confirmation of his faith in the indigenous culture of the Hawaiian Islands. In himself and in other Hawaiians, he came to feel, stirred the collective unconscious of his ancestors. He became more and more spiritual in his inclinations. Walter Ritte mentions how he and George "simply followed our instincts... wherever they led us, we trusted them." In a letter to Emmett Aluli, Helm wrote: "Listen carefully to your inner voices and observe without personal bias the inner pulse of mankind..."

Helm and the PKA kept moving. Through their efforts, archaeological surveys were being conducted on Kahoolawe. Many *heiaus* (religious shrines) were found. Also found were petroglyphs and numerous artifacts. The PKA filed suits against the Navy. Helm, Ritte, Aluli, and others sought out "every kupuna elder on every island, teamed up with lawyers, Hawaiian scholars, and religious experts, to take on the Sisyphean task of piecing together the remnants of a shattered culture.

The concept "aloha aina" was alive again. Hawaiian gods—buried in the rocks by Christian missionaries—were, so to speak, alive again. Ohana members spoke not only of Pele, but also Kanaloa, Kane, Lono, and Ku.

And a trip to Kahoolawe had started it all.

Music, too, was a key to George Helm's spirituality, and

"Lend me the stone strength of the past
and I will lend you
The wings of the future, for I have
them."

"To the Rock That Will be a Cornerstone"
Robinson Jeffers

the music that opened the door to the Hawaiian culture also brought young and old Hawaiians together. One day, Helm and Ritte went to Keanae, a *very* Hawaiian place on the Hana side of Maui, to speak before a group of elderly Hawaiians. Aluli had arranged the meeting. When the trio entered the church, wearing ti-leaf headbands around their long hair and ti leaves wrapped around their ankles, the people were immediately turned off to those "hippies," those "radicals." The group spoke among themselves in Hawaiian—ostracizing them. But after Helm played and sang some old Hawaiian songs ("to warm them up," Aluli says), the old people were all in tears and ready to listen. Ritte and Aluli shared their *mana'o*, speaking as young Hawaiians who were simply trying to find their lost culture by following not just their hearts but their *na'au* (gut feelings). Helm also spoke. At one point he told his audience straight: "You put us down for our not being able to speak Hawaiian. *You* are the reason we cannot speak Hawaiian and have to go buy it at the university." By the time the three were done, the Keanae people told them, "You boys are not radicals, you are *hui o ho'oponopono,* those who will set things right."

Helm also set things right on the home front. Ritte and Aluli, despite being linked in everyone's mind because of the initial landing, never got along. "Emmett's too methodical," Ritte would say. "He wants to weigh the pros and cons. With me and George, we just went and did it." Aluli states, "One of George's favorite lines was, 'for every action there's a reaction.' Before I move, I check gut reactions first—mine, or anybody's, to figure the counter-reactions."

Helm kept the two together. He spent much of his time bringing and keeping people together. He could sit and talk with the old, run and play with the young. Whether singing or speaking, Helm always seemed to hit the right notes. The natural, easy-going warmth that characterized his approach, and the fact that he *did his homework* made whatever he'd say ring true. People listened to him. People believed him. And believed in him. George Jarrett Helm, Jr., had become the

Christmas party on Molokai.

Photo courtesy of the PKO

voice and soul of the body politic, expressing the collective angst of the disenfranchised. "You talk grass roots, Kumu," a friend said in a letter. "Don't fail them now."

By January, 1977, the Helm-led PKO (Aunty Edith said, "You're not an association, you are *'ohana* (family).") was making a big impact on the state. Polls showed that two-thirds of Hawaii's population wanted the bombing of Kahoolawe halted and the island returned to the people of Hawaii. Around this time Helm began receiving disturbing phone calls. Anonymous callers suggested he not rock the boat, that too many were benefitting from "politics as usual." But Helm felt too deeply that too many people—especially Hawaiians—were suffering *because* people refused to rock the boat. Hawaiians were underrepresented in professional jobs, overrepresented in prisons and on welfare rolls. People were hurting. Therefore, for Helm there was no stopping.

The Kahoolawe issue was building toward a crescendo. The archaeological survey, which had covered 4,100 acres, 14% of the island's total land area, had uncovered thirty sites and all but one of them were deemed eligible for the National Register of Historic Places. In response to these findings Emmett Aluli said in a statement that they had been trying to tell people about these sites for months but it took a group of non-Hawaiians to verify these findings for anyone to listen. PKO members found it reprehensible that the Navy would continue the bombing and not only ignore the wishes of a large segment of Hawaii's population but also ignore the value of these findings and continue bombing the remnants of their overrun culture. Walter Ritte was especially disturbed and wanted to act in response. Helm felt the same.

They very quietly arranged for another landing on Kahoolawe in late January. If word got out that they were planning to land, the Navy would stop them and perhaps confiscate the boat. On January 30, five men landed: Helm, Ritte, Richard Sawyer, Charles Warrington, and Francis Kauhane. The plan was that Ritte and Sawyer would stay indefinitely. While those

"We're not going to do away with the car. We just want open space for our kids."

two set up camp, the other three hiked around the northeast end of the island for a day before giving themselves up to the Coast Guard. Helm made it his job to gather support to put an end, once and for all, to the bombing. Previously, he had resisted "working within the system," distrustful as he was of politicians. But the urgency of the situation compelled him to take the political route. Helm met with legislators, worked with a legislative committee that was formed to look into the Kahoolawe matter.

He also used the media. Along with other Ohana members, Helm gave interviews, churned out press releases, appeared on radio talk shows. On Ron Jacob's show on radio station KKUA—the number one show on the air—Helm stated angrily, breathing hard between phrases:

> When I walk down to Kohala, and I walk house to house in Hana, and I walk house to house in Molokai, I go down to Waimanalo and Nanakuli, and I see all the Hawaiian people, I get insulted at the easy display of ignorance by the politicians. They're using statistics to define the problems and they ain't gonna know the problem until they sit down and look [the people] in the eye.... it takes a lot of stripping away.

The bombing continued. Helm and others were enraged when the Navy stated that no one was on the island. Helm had Mrs. Ritte and Mrs. Sawyer, both pregnant, to comfort. He stepped up his campaign.

After the arraignment of the two other Kahoolawe trespassers on February 10, Helm led a group of Ohana members on a march to the State Capital. There they gathered in circle to *pule* (pray). Helm stated, "If God can hear our prayers, how come the politicians cannot?"

Apparently some heard, for on February 11, Helm spoke before the State House. This was an unprecedented event. No non-member had ever been allowed to address the legislature before, but after representatives Henry Peters and Jan Yuen (who had asked him to speak) give other House members assurances that it would not set a precedent, the House rules were temporarily suspended. Helm moved his audience, some of them to tears, and the House quickly introduced and adopted a resolution to have the bombing stopped.

Then it was on to Washington, D.C. On February 14, Helm, along with PKO member Francis Kauhane, left for the nation's capital to take the matter up with President Jimmy Carter. They had sent a telegram to him on February 2 and had received no response. Carter, apparently, was vacationing in Plains, Georgia. Also, three-fourths of Hawaii's delegation, all except Senator Spark Matsunaga, were in Hawaii being briefed on the Kahoolawe issue by the U.S. Navy. (The Navy had arranged for Hawaii's Congressional delegation to see what they were doing on Kahoolawe. They took Senator Dan Inouye and congressmen Cec Heftel and Dan Akaka to the island. *Hawaii Observer* reporter Pam Smith, who went with the group, called it "Kahoolawe Whitewash." She wrote of how the Navy steered the delegation towards the worst areas, showing them that nothing could grow, that the soil was useless. Eight by tens of Naval commanders were also handed out to all of those there. The Navy gave the group a little demonstration. According to Smith, "F4 jets dropped 27 Mark 76's—dummy bombs with an explosive device the size of a 12-gauge shotgun shell" rather than the usual live 500-pound bombs. The congressional party went away very satisfied with the demonstration and expressed thanks to the Navy for accommodating them.)

Meanwhile, Helm and Kauhane were being frustrated by the bureaucratic labyrinth. Inouye, the one congressman who could have opened doors for them, was not around. His staff was no help. When the two finally secured an appointment with Assistant Secretary of Defense Tom Ross, Ross confessed he was ignorant of the issue and would have to review it. No one seemed to know anything about Kahoolawe or about anything to do with Hawaiians, for that matter. Hawaiians did not exist in the nation's capital, Helm and Kauhane discovered. They returned home outraged.

The PKO planned a mass invasion of Kahoolawe. This was set for February 20. The night before, about a hundred Ohana members gathered at Makena Beach on Maui. Word leaked out to the Coast Guard and the invasion was called off because of fears that boats would be confiscated. Finally, ten people, all picked secretly by Helm, made the landing. All but two were arrested by the hundred marines dispatched to track them down. The two who weren't caught managed the seven-mile swim back to Maui. No contact had been made with Ritte and Sawyer.

A momentary respite was in order. On February 26, Helm flew to Molokai to attend the first birthday party for his nephew, the son of Adolph and Corene. Many among the 800 gathered at the family house in Kalamaula said he sang beautifully that night, that his voice was better than ever. But his troubles were with him. He felt responsible for Ritte and Sawyer, who were on Kahoolawe, risking their lives. He spent much of the evening comforting Zennie, Richard Sawyer's wife. A few days earlier he had told members of his immediate family that threats might be made on their lives and that in a short while he was going to "break something big." Though pressed for facts, Helm refused to say much more than that he was about to expose high-level political corruption. (He had been gathering information regarding misuse of land. From county workers in Maui, for example, he learned about water being diverted from Hana, where many Hawaiians live, to cane fields owned by Alexander and Baldwin and places like Wailea and Makena where resort developments were planned. With the help of the many sources he had cultivated in his inter-island travels, he learned how behind-the-scenes development decisions were being made.)

By this time the Protect Kahoolawe Ohana had grown into a rather large organization, partly because of the organizing talents of Helm and other Ohana members, and partly because of the media attention the whole Kahoolawe issue had attracted. However, the spiritual aspect of the struggle, which guided founding members, was lost on many of the newcomers. (Some of them wanted to "work within the system." Some were simply more anti-military than pro *aloha 'aina*. Women members complained about the *macho-ness* of the men who didn't want any females going to Kahoolawe illegally. The PKO was having growing pains.) Still, the energy of new members was sorely needed and welcomed for the whirlwind of activity was taking its toll. "They all looked so weary, drained," a female Ohana member recalls. "It was pathetic."

Helm seemed to be holding up well under the strain, but the Kahoolawe issue obsessed him and made him much more serious. Though he still made people laugh—he never lost his touch for seeing the humor in just about everything—his humor had definite dark undertones. In PKO meetings Helm chided those who made wisecracks. No more fun and games. And when he spoke or sang, the coloration in his tones suggested that Helm was attuned to something deep within. At Makena, on the night before the mass invasion attempt, after Ohana members gathered in a circle to *pule,* he spoke with such passion, such intensity, that some there felt his time was near, that even *he* knew he was going to die. (One friend clearly remembers him stating, around this time, "What I'm doing is going to cost me my life.")

Still, many others could not understand his urgency. There were moments of doubt. "Am I the only one who feels this way?" he stated to a friend at the Gold Coin restaurant where he continued to perform his music. (Some wondered how Helm could continue performing during those trying times. On the other hand, others feel, how could he not? Music seemed to be the constant, the sustenance, the well which he drew from, a well dug deep into the *'aina.*)

On March 1, Helm went over to Bishop Museum to talk to anthropologist Kenneth Emory, Edith MacKenzie, Elly Williamson, and Auntie Edith Kanakaole. Their conversation (with Helm doing most of the talking) covered a lot of areas, a significant part of which dealt with the god Lono. (Lono-

"Kahoolawe can teach the rest of the world Aloha 'Aina and save us from becoming evolutionary dropouts."

i-ka-makahiki, according to Hawaiian scholars and *kupuna,* was a great chief elevated to the status of god largely because of superhuman deeds. Legend has it that one day this same chief left Hawaii for Tahiti, vowing to return. He never did. When Captain James Cook arrived in 1779 to the shores of Kealakekua Bay, he was mistakenly identified as the god Lono, largely because the masts of his ships resembled Lono's tapa banner insignia. Cook was later killed on the shores of the same bay and supposedly partially eaten.) Helm saw Lono-i-ka-makahiki—god of agriculture, storm rain, and music—as a benevolent god and wanted to perform a *ho'okupu* in his honor. Helm had heard his Auntie Apolonia Day talk of an ancestor by the name of Lono-i-ka-makahiki and thought he may be a descendant of Lono and had been researching his genealogy in an attempt to confirm this. (Rubellite Kawena Johnson, a noted Hawaiian scholar, once told Helm that they were looking for the same thing—she through the *Kumulipo,* the ancient Hawaiian creation chant, he through Kahoolawe—*Lono-i-ka-makahiki.* At Bishop Museum, Helm told Emory and the others that a woman had approached him when he was on the Big Island and told him, cryptically, "They're gonna take Lono-i-ka-makahiki away from you guys." In a later incident someone approached Helm and said, "You're gonna die a violent death." Helm couldn't help but snicker when he spoke of these incidents. "Here we go again," he said, "Lono-i-ka-makahiki."

Helm later stated he believed the time of Lono had come again, that Lono was to return, not in the form of a god, but in *concept.* The time of Ku, the god of war, was over, and Lono would return, 200 years after Cook, in the spirit of *aloha 'aina.* "Kahoolawe can teach the rest of the world *aloha 'aina* and save us from becoming evolutionary dropouts."

Then there were dreams. Signs. After the initial landing, Helm never went to Kahoolawe without some kind of sign, whether from a dream or from the natural world. Nor without checking with various *kupuna.* Psychoanalyst Jung emphasized the meaningfulness of dreams in everyday life. So did the kupuna Helm talked to. Helm believed that dreams were a way of being attuned to the *collective unconscious* through which his ancestors spoke. So when Helm had a dream about Walter Ritte—something vague about shoes, the tying of shoelaces, and a baby—he did not take it lightly.

Helm quickly sought out advice. By coincidence, others were having dreams that related to Kahoolawe. Francis Kauhane had dreamt that Ritte and Sawyer were in danger. *Kahuna* Morrnah Simeona dreamt that Kahoolawe had been washed over by gigantic waves. She told Helm to go get Walter and Richard. Others had dreams of some kind of danger.

And there were signs. During this time there had been for a few days a halo around the moon, caused by ice crystals in the earth's upper stratosphere. This usually portends a storm. Scientific explanations notwithstanding, this phenomena seemed ominous. *Kahuna* Emma de Fries said it foretold some kind of upheaval or cataclysm and is said to have warned Helm not to go to Kahoolawe. Helm sought out other *kupuna.* Most foresaw some kind of danger. Some said go, some said don't go. Helm decided to go.

He quietly made arrangements to go to Kahoolawe to get Ritte and Sawyer off the island. His friends were in possible danger and he felt that that was reason enough to go. Helm asked Billy Mitchell, an Ohana member who had been working with the legislative committee formed to look into the Kahoolawe matter, to help with arrangements for a backup boat and flew on over to Maui.

The attempt to get on Kahoolawe on Thursday night, March 4, failed. The captain of the boat taking them over "chickened out" and turned around when he thought he saw a Coast Guard cutter. (It turned out to be a barge.) Visibly upset, Helm spent the night at a house in Kihei and early the next morning went over to Hana to seek aid from, in his words, "My ohana."

After talking to friends in Hana, Helm ended up at Kimo Mitchell's Keanae home. (Kimo Mitchell and Sluggo Hahn had a boat and had helped with their last illegal landing.) Helm told those who had gathered there that he was sure Ritte and Sawyer were in danger, Helm said he needed their assistance. Mitchell and Hahn gave their okay and they began packing. Soon they were on their way. *(For a full account of this day in Hana, see* "Kimo Mitchell" *story.)*

Again Helm ended up in Kihei, this time with a different crew. Billy Mitchell had arrived with Polo Simeona, a Honolulu fireman who was to provide the back-up boat. Because Billy Mitchell was a skilled waterman, Helm asked him to go along with him to the island. (Earlier Helm had asked Kimo Mitchell—no relation to Billy—to go with him because he too was skilled in the water. Kimo said okay.) After resting a while, the crew did their final packing. Helm gave girlfriend Leimomi Apoliona his wallet. He had earlier asked her to fly to Maui to be with him. He said he needed someone to hold his wallet because there was "nothing to buy on Kahoolawe." With his humor intact, he left. At 2:30 a.m. Saturday morning the crew left on the boat for Kahoolawe. They were to arrive a half hour later.

Helm was exhausted. On the way to Kihei, he had slept on the boat in uncomfortable positions. For a while he slept with his head resting against a fuel tank. But now he was alert. As they neared the island, they saw what seemed to be a Coast Guard helicopter approaching from a distance. Someone said, "Hit it," and George Helm, Kimo Mitchell, and Billy Mitchell jumped into the water with their two surfboards, an inner tube, and their supplies, carefully wrapped in plastic bags.

The three, according to Billy Mitchell, could not find Ritte and Sawyer, though Helm knew exactly where the base camp was. Ritte and Sawyer had apparently left the base camp near Keheohala Point and had gone to Pedro's Bay in search of food and water.

There they found food and what they interpreted to be a sign. Baby goats began approaching them and pretty soon they found themselves saddled with a bunch of baby goats that were in dire need of nourishment. Ritte and Sawyer viewed these goats as gifts from the island and decided they would give themselves up in order to save them. After trying to be spotted for two days, a Coast Guard helicopter finally picked up the two.

Meanwhile, not knowing Ritte and Sawyer were off the island, the three others continued their search. According to Billy Mitchell, Helm seemed to be "wracked by spirits." At times he spoke lucidly, educating Kimo and Billy about the island. Other times he would fall down into sleep and the other two would have a hard time waking him up. This pattern continued all through that Saturday.

The pickup boat, scheduled for 11 p.m. that night, did not arrive. (It had sunk back in Kihei, its plugs were all out. Crew members were scrambling around for another boat. Polo Simeona, the Honolulu fireman who was to have provided a back-up boat, had left earlier that day.) A few hours later, at about 3 a.m. Sunday morning, the three supposedly entered the high surf on two surfboards in an effort to get to Maui, or Molokini, a tiny crescent shaped island two miles off Maui's Makena coastline. Helm is said to have suffered a slight gash on his forehead upon entering.

Helm and Kimo Mitchell disappeared. Billy Mitchell, the lone survivor, says he last saw the other two near Molokini, struggling in the surf, and paddled back to Kahoolawe to get help.

Back on Kahoolawe, he hiked the island barefoot for a day, looking for help. A day later he came across some marines camped at a firing range. He was transported off the island. While on the helicopter he told military officials that two friends were lost in the waters off Kahoolawe. After convincing them he wasn't lying, and after the news spread through-[illegible] the islands, a collective effort of the U.S. military, the [illegible], friends, family, watermen, and fire rescue specialists [illegible]nched a search for two of Hawaii's favorite sons, George Helm and Kimo Mitchell.

Why did Helm and the two Mitchell's leave the relative safety of land to enter extremely rough waters? Gale warnings were in effect. It is said that twenty-foot waves were hitting Kahoolawe. Billy Mitchell gave the media and the family and friends of the missing two these conflicting reasons: 1) lack of food and water; 2) to light a bonfire on Molokini; 3) to get Helm off the island because he was so wracked by spirits that the others felt he would have died had they stayed.

Those close to the two say they could have easily survived on the island. Kimo's father, Harry Mitchell, says that coconuts are constantly washed ashore, that Kimo, a child of the land, knew how to survive in such conditions. Friends of Helm say he loved the island, thought of it as a baby, and knew Kahoolawe well enough to know where water and food might be. Crew members say they would have returned, they would have gotten another boat.

The pieces don't fit together, many say. Yet, what does fit, for Helm at least, is a death at sea. If one were to look at a map of Maui, as it faces Kahoolawe (see Map 2), Maui does take on the shape of a mother, full breasted, looking longingly at her child (Kahoolawe is fetus-shaped). The PKO, then, functions as the umbilical cord trying to provide life to the unnurtured island. The surrounding ocean is the womb. Looking at it this way, it fits, it all fits, especially when one reads a journal entry written by George Helm long before his disappearance:

> *I dreamt of being in the ocean as if I was a part of it, like I belonged in the water—it gave me content[ment] and I felt no frustration... Konani was it the dream... kind of reminds me of my mother... was this a dream... to return to my mother's womb—warm, secured, fearless, and contented.*

Dreams. Prophesies. *George Jarrett Helm, Jr., spokesman for generations, traveled to and from Kahoolawe to see them fulfilled.*

"The feelings I'm presently with is described as a desire to be with someone who really cares to help clarify the individual confusion we're all victims of. Youth and not enough years prolong the wanting to grab hold of someone. I would venture to say that when one finally understands that desire he or she would be without the need to have someone. At times the road is a lonely one and a very long one. I will continue to pursue the course for as long as it will take me to understand the strange primitive or primary instincts."

Alexis Higdon

Originally published in 1954 in the "Hawaii Weekly" section of the Honolulu Advertiser, *this story lauds the accomplishments of Helm's father, George, Sr. as a homestead farmer.*

Molokai Miracle

Fortunato Teho

This is the story of 39-year-old George Helm, Maui-born German-Hawaiian who in the past six months has established a farm on Hawaiian Homes Commission (HHC) land at Kalamaula, Molokai, that has become the envy of all other homesteaders on the Friendly Isle.

The farm, according to Molokai Commissioner Norman B. McGuire, is the first in HHC annals to fulfill the terms of the lease and law and the purpose of the rehabilitation act.

The HHC act, passed in July 9, 1921, was an experiment in the controlled economic rehabilitation of the rapidly disappearing Hawaiian race. Under the act each qualified homesteader is given a 99-year lease on a certain tract of land from which he is expected to make a living full time.

Now for a little background. Mr. Helm applied for a homestead in 1942, but it was not until 1950 that his application was approved and with it a $3,000 loan with which he managed to build a modest three-bedroom home. Using mostly surplus materials, and by doing most of the carpentry, painting and plumbing himself with the assistance of his wife, Melanie, he completed the job with an expenditure of only $2,300. With the balance he paid off $700 indebtedness on the land contracted by the former leaseholder.

An expert tractor operator Mr. Helm followed jobs wherever he could find them, some of which took him away at times from his growing family. As his family increased he found it harder to provide for its necessities and at times he had to seek assistance from welfare.

About six months ago he decided to give up the idea of working for others and spend his full time working for himself. The five acres adjoining his home had been neglected and most of it overgrown with kiawe and other wild brush. To make the situation worse, previous to his occupancy, people had used the area as a rubbish site.

With only a cane knife and pickax he began the arduous

and backbreaking job of clearing the land for planting. He burned most of the rubbish and dug and leveled the area with hand tools. It was a monumental task on which he spent countless hours. He and his family were often at it long before sunup and until late after sundown. After nearly two months of continuous labor, which included Sundays and holidays, Mr. Helm was finally able to get his land in condition for planting.

Having had no previous experience in farming, he sought and obtained the assistance of Molokai's county extension agent, Fuyuki Okumura. Mr. Okumura cheerfully cooperated and became his guide and adviser. He was told what, when, where and how to plant his farm so as to take advantage of existing conditions and at the same time practice the principles of balanced farming.

Since the area is hot and exposed to drying winds, he was told to use windbreaks and to practice mulching in order to conserve irrigation water. To lessen the effect of winds he built a windbreak of coconut fronds. He also used the fronds, of which there was a great abundance in a nearby coconut grove, for mulching around his crops.

Fresh irrigation water was supplied by the HHC at 20 cents per 1,000 gallons. To cut down his expenses he dug a 10-foot well which daily supplied 24,000 gallons of brackish water with a salt content of from 50 to 60 grains. For the more tolerant crops he used this water straight, but had to flush out the accumulated salt with fresh water once in every 10 irrigations. For the less tolerant plants he used a mixture of fresh and brackish water. All in all he found that this system, plus mulching, cut his water bill as much as 50 per cent.

Crops which are sensitive to direct sunshine, such as taro and lettuce, were grown in the shade of trees which served also to shield the heat from his rabbitry, chicken coops and pig pen.

The first planting produced a bountiful harvest of string beans, tomatoes, carrots, radishes, Chinese peas, kohlrabi, spinach, turnips, peppers, onions and watermelons. All this was grown with practically no fertilizer because of the fertile soil.

There was already a market for his produce because fresh vegetables are scarce on the island. Customers came on the average of about a dozen a day and were given the privilege of picking their produce. From the first planting Mr. Helm grossed about $800 and the figure would have been larger had not some of the vegetables been given away to neighbors and friends.

Because of the fine example he set, Mr. Helm was recently able to obtain a $2,000 loan from the HHC to purchase equipment to further assist him in his farming operations.

Although short of funds, the HHC was able to make this loan, the first of its kind in HHC history, through the collective efforts of the Kauai, Oahu and Molokai commissions.

With their experience, and with assurances of help from farm experts, the Helms are planning on greater things and hope to develop their farm into a model for others to follow.

People stop by and offer words of encouragement and advice and follow the progress of the Helms with interest and pride. For did they not contribute to the couple's welfare by offering them a hoe, a rake or some other article or piece of equipment which they could spare?

It is interesting to note that the first demonstration farm on Molokai was started in this area in 1922, one year after the passage of the HHC act. But it took 32 years before any of the homesteaders could prove that the project was practical and could be made self-supporting.

Here is an outstanding example of what determination and perserverance can do for those who will not be discouraged by seemingly insurmountable odds.

Kahoolawe: Chants, Legends, Poems, Stories by Children of Maui

Compiled by Wayne Westlake

Kahoolawe once was a piece of coral
deep in the sea with seaweeds growing over it,
and fishes that swam around it,
Until one day the coral exploded
and became an island.
Birds came and dropped seeds on the island.
The seeds grew and the island came alive.

Kahoolawe now is an island with trees growing,
and birds that fly over it
and people that bomb it.

Ruth Nakamura. Grade 5

"E Mau" was a favorite song of George Helm's, one that he often quoted. Written in 1941, it preaches aloha ‘aina.

E Mau

Alvin Kaleolani Isaacs, Sr.

E mau ko kakou lahui, e ho‘omau.
E mau ko kakou ’olelo, e ho’omau.
E mau ka hana pono o ka ’aina
I mau ka ea o ka ’aina i ka pono.
I ka pono—o ka ’aina!!

Ho’oulu ka pono o ka ’aina, e ho’oulu.
Ho’ola ka nani o ka ’aina, e ho’ola.
Ho’ola la, Ho’oulu la, a ho’olaha
I mau ka ea o ka ’aina i ka pono.
I ka pono—o ka ’aina!!

Let's Strive

Alvin Kaleolani Isaacs, Sr.

Let's strive to keep our nation alive, let's strive.
Let's strive to keep our language alive, let's strive.
Let's strive to preserve the good of the islands
So that righteousness may continue to be with us.
All that's good—in the islands!!

Build the greatness of Hawai'i, build them.
Restore the goodness of the islands, restore them.
Restore!! Build, and sustain them throughout the world
So that righteousness will fill the land once again.
Every good—in the islands!!

Alexis Higdon

Hawaiian Soul

Words and Music by Jon Osorio, Randy Borden

*Dedicated to the memory
of George Helm*

I can recall the way
your voice would fill the room
and we would all be stilled
by your melody
but now your voice is gone
and to the sea belongs
all of the gentle songs
that you had harbored

Hawaiian soul
how could you leave us
You've not been lost at sea
you're only wandering

Hawaiian Soul
we sing your melody
and send them out to sea
You know the harmony

They say before you left
to seek your destiny
that older voices called
and drowned your laughter
but I believe you knew
what you would have to be
a beacon in the storm
to guide us after

Liner Notes for *Islands*

"Molokai Sweet Home" was easily my favorite new song of 1983, which explains why two months before the Hoku awards I wrote in the Honolulu Advertiser: "My bet to win the Hoku for song of the year is 'Molokai Sweet Home,' by Malani Bilyeu." That also explains why, when Malani asked, I was pleased to volunteer a few lines for his impressive first album.

"Molokai Sweet Home" is such a lovely song that it will be played, performed and just hum-mumbled the way lots of folks do for years. It has the sound of a classic Hawaiian song. Honest emotions when converted to an art form by a talented and conscientious artist have a way of becoming classic simply because they strike a shared cord that is finely tuned in the human heart.

In this case, Malani—his name means "Messenger from Heaven"—had been touring the Mainland with Kalapana for almost four years. He was missing Hawaii tremendously when he heard that his "idol," George Helm, had died back home. Malani was moved to write a song in George's honor and the result was "Molokai."

Don Chapman, columnist
The Honolulu Advertiser

Molokai Sweet Home

Malani Bilyeu

I'll feel your evening breeze tonight
        Moloka'i I'm longing for your laughter
I'll gaze upon your silent shore
        and reminisce that sweet embrace of ginger
As New York City walls closed in
        I longed for the touch of an island
    Moloka'i, Moloka'i—sweet home

So tutu rest your weary eyes
        I've missed your smiles and lullabyes in the evening time
It's been so long since I've been home
        I miss the morning sunrise of the countryside
I've gone so far to find my way
        this time I think I'll stay with an island
    Moloka'i, Moloka'i—sweet home

Ballad of George Helm

Malani Bilyeu

1. He was born a son of Moloka'i
   Hawaiian Pride and strong in mind
   It seems that it was yesterday
   when we met and there was no goodbye

2. He sang his songs of Island Life
   The people and the sky of blue
   His voice could reach within your soul
   he gave his heart and tears to me and you
   remember him a native son so true

(Chorus:)

Why does the sun shine bright
George has gone and it don't seem right
Where has the music gone
He left us with an empty song

3. His message reads to save the land
   Islands in the sun are few
   Existence is the earth you stand
   He left it up to me and up to you
   remember him a native son so true

(Repeat Chorus)

How Kahoolawe Became the Smallest Island

Calvin Tasaka. Grade 5

Kahoolawe was once a big island but now real small you know. Why came small? Kahoolawe came small because some billy goat hit the mountains down and the hammerhead shark when pound all the edges down. Everytime dirt come down the clams swallow the dirt and go to the deepest part in the Pacific Ocean and spit the dirt out. That's how Kahoolawe got so small.

Ed Greevy

George Helm

'Ilima Pi'ianai'a

He punahele no 'oe na ka makua. This first line of a song which is dear to George Helm says that you are a favorite of the generation before. In the fall George had heard the song and spent a few afternoons working on it until he could include it in his repertoire. There were few contemporary songs which George sang. His appreciation centered on songs which had been written during the first half of this century and embodied what George called "Hawaiian Soul."

He found his musical gift inspired through our elder musicians and composers. The Isaacs family, Andy Cummings, David Nape, Alfred Alohikea and Lena Machado were among his favorites, and through their Hawaiian Soul he came to understand the political awareness, the crying hurt and the unspoken dignity of the Hawaiians of the 1920s, 1930s and 1940s. All of these qualities—as well as those of passion and humor—are found in Hawaiian songs which most young contemporary Hawaiian musicians ignore in an attempt to develop a new sound.

George Helm the musician is a little known individual in comparison to George Helm the "activist" and one of the prime movers in Hawaiian political consciousness. But through his music older Hawaiians were touched in the depths of their *na'au,* their guts, and understood what George was about. Whenever he played his guitar and sang in public, he always looked for gray heads, and when he found them he sang for them.

The loss of George at sea is affecting Hawaiians of all ages and of many different interests. The internal communication system of the Hawaiian community is buzzing. Contacts are being made among individuals who heretofore have not had much in common, or so they thought. The reactions to the events surrounding George's loss range from disbelief to quiet acceptance. One of the basic questions is: why did this happen? The answer shall forever remain with George.

In his endeavors over the past year and a half, George has

touched more Hawaiians than any other individual. He has had contact with many of the various interest groups within the Hawaiian community. He has been respected, if not always agreed with, and has always offered to kokua in whatever way he could. One of his goals has been to bring the community together and to help individuals understand that for Hawaiians the long-range objective is the same: to be Hawaiian above rather than under ground.

One of the most important and critical facets of George's being is that he has bridged gaps between the old and the contemporary. His understanding of the continuous and timeless stream of things Hawaiian is unequaled by his peers. In George was a person of two worlds or two ages—the purely Hawaiian values before 1778 and the non-Hawaiian values imposed over the past two centuries. There have been, of course, deep conflicts generated within George, and he has felt the pains from such conflicts. But he has also been able to run with the younger Hawaiians and sit with the older ones.

For younger Hawaiians George has very capably articulated many of their frustrations and has been instrumental in laying out strategies in their effort to be heard. He has set direction, connected different factions and shown that there is indeed Hawaiian Soul. From older Hawaiians he has learned. He has spent many hours listening as remembered knowledge was shared with him and as advice was administered to him.

As busy as he was, George always found the time to spend with individuals and to go to the shore. He was gentle and solicitous in his care for other people. When he asked, "How you, you okay?", he really wanted to know. And if you weren't okay, his gentleness and concern somehow made you a little more okay. When he himself was troubled or needed to meditate or had to work something out, he went to the ocean. From the ocean he would gain strength and calmness. It was never a surprise when George said, "Let's go to the shore," at any time of day or night. There he would go off by himself for awhile, and when he had worked things out he would come back to us with a renewed spirit.

The literal translation of the contemporary name of Kahoolawe is "the carrying away by currents." The traditional name of the Island is Kohe Malamalama o Kanaloa, "the shining vagina of Kanaloa." Kanaloa is our god of the sea. For a people who are so much of the sea, being lost at sea is a sweet burial.

(The name Kohe Malamalama o Kanaloa signifies that Hawaiians recognize Kahoolawe as a sacred place where Kanaloa is an ocean person and in his role as the god of the sea was received, obtained resuscitation, and was re-energized. Kohe in this sense refers to a place which receives and nourishes. Malamalama is a contemporary contraction of malama malama, to take care of.)

IN MEMORY OF GEORGE HELM, A TRUE HAWAIIAN WHO LOVED THE AINA, PEOPLE, AND MUSIC.

Where does the sun set?
Is it here? Is it there?
I know it was somewhere.

Perhaps a storm came
and the stream
washed it away.

Perhaps the mountains
came down on us
and covered it all up.

Maybe it was the kai
Maybe the kai came up
and flooded the valleys
and on its way back
wen hapai everything
and take it all out to sea.

Nah, brah
it wasn't any of these things
The storm was greed
swelling like a dammed-up stream
making ready to overrun
and wash away.

And the mountains that crumbled
did so because of absence
    absence from the land
    absence from the kai
    absence from the people
    absence from the mana.

And we know what the wave was!
    Genocide.
Flooding the valleys
and stripping the limu clean
from the rocks
Sweeping away the ʻopae
from the streams
the ulu from the land
and the maoli from the earth.

So . . . ah . . . tell me brah
    where does the sun set?
Is it here?
    Is it there?
Tell me
    Where do I take Granpa's bones?

A Chant to Kahoolawe

Lester Nakamoto. Grade 5

Kahoolawe the home of Monsters
once the most beautiful island in Hawaii.
We the children of Hawaii want to help you, but
we are unable to.
The Monsters overpower our Kahunas.
The bravest men are killed.
Our Gods are helpless against the Monsters.
Goodbye forever Kahoolawe.

Kahoolawe once was a beautiful lady
dancing in the night.
Some nights she was frightened
but kept dancing on all night.

Joy Blakeslee. Grade 5

Kahoolawe now is a floating bomb.
They think it will go off about 300 years from now.
If you go about 30 feet away you can hear it ticking.
The bomb has been ticking away for 200 years.

Ellen Enoki. Grade 5

"*Call me a radical for I refuse to remain idle. I will not have the foreigner prostitute the soul of my being, and I will not make a whore out of my soul (my culture).*"

January 30th – 1977 I have my Thought you have your thought
Simple fact are difficult for you

Simply .... the reason is I'm a Hawaiian and I'm inspirited. The soul of my kupuna. It is my moral responsibility to attempt an ending to this desecration of our sacred aina, Kohe malamalama o Kanaloa, for each bomb dropped adds further injury to an already wounded soul.

The truth is, there is man and there is environment — one does not supersede the other — the breath in man is the breath on land — man maintains land, air, and ocean, it maintains man. Therefore aina is sacred — The church of life is not a building — it is the open sky, the surrounding ocean, the beautiful soil. My duty is to protect the giver of life —

What is National Defense when what is being destroyed is the very thing being defended — the sacred land of (Hawaii) America.

E mau ko kakou lahui e ho‘omau.
Ho‘oulu ka pono o ka ‘aina e Ho‘oulu
Hoola ka nani o ka ‘aina e Ho‘ola
E MAU KE EA O KA ‘AINA I KA PONO
—Alvin Isaacs, Sr.

Personal Statement—Reasons for Fourth Occupation of Kahoolawe

55

George Helm

January 30, 1977

I have my thoughts, you have your thoughts, simple for me, difficult for you. Simply . . . the reason is . . . I am a Hawaiian and I've inherited the soul of my kupuna. It is my moral responsibility to attempt an ending to this desecration of our sacred ‘aina, Kohe Malamalama o Kanaloa, for each bomb dropped adds further injury to an already wounded soul.

The truth is, there is man and there is environment. One does not supercede the other. The breath in man is the breath of Papa (the earth). Man is merely the caretaker of the land that maintains his life and nourishes his soul. Therefore, ‘aina is sacred. The church of life is not in a building, it is the open sky, the surrounding ocean, the beautiful soil. My duty is to protect Mother Earth, who gives me life. And to give thanks with humility as well as ask forgiveness for the arrogance and insensitivity of man.

What is national defense when what is being destroyed is the very thing the military is entrusted to defend, the sacred land of (Hawai‘i) America. The spirit of pride is left uncultivated, without truth and without meaning for the keiki o ka ‘aina, cut off from the land as a fetus is cut off from his mother. National defense is indefensible in terms of the loss of pride for many of the citizens of Hawai‘i-nei. Call me radical for I refuse to remain idle. I will not have the foreigner prostitute the soul of my being, and I will not make a whore out of my soul (my culture).

All the archaeological discoveries, incredibly, are not enough cause, it seems, for the federal government to respect the sacredness of history. This continued disregard of our seriousness, this refusal to give credibility to the Hawaiian culture based on Aloha ‘Aina, forces me to protest.

Lehua Hough. Grade 4

A beautiful Woman, she has beautiful
black hair, and a slender body, but
she has been cursed by an evil
Kahuna that has given her an evil mind. One
day when she was walking through the
forest she saw a beautiful red bird, but
without even thinking she walked up to it very
silently and killed it. When seeing the blood on
her finger she fainted. Then the Kahuna
thought she was dead and threw her in the
ocean. From that day on nobody has ever
gone back to the island that Kahoolawe
lived on.

Poem for George Helm
Aloha Week 1980

Eric Chock

I was in love with the word "aloha"
Even though I heard it over and over
I let the syllables ring in my ears
and I believed the king with outstretched hand
was welcoming everyone who wanted to live here
And I ignored the spear in his left hand
believing instead my fellow humans
and their love for these islands in the world
which allow us to rest from the currents
and moods of that vast ocean from which we all came
But George Helm's body is back in that ocean
I want to believe in the greatness of his spirit
that he still feels the meaning of that word
which is getting so hard to say

I thought there was hope for the word "aloha"
I believed when they said there are ways
in this modern technological world Oahu alone
could hold a million people
And we would become the Great Crossroads of the Pacific
if we used our native aloha spirit
our friendly wahines and our ancient hulas
They showed us our enormous potential
and we learned to love it
like a man who loves some thing in gold or silver
But these islands are made of lava and trees and sand
A man learns to swim with the ocean
and when he's tired he begins to search
for what he loves, for what will sustain him
George Helm is lost at sea
The bombing practice continues on Kahoolawe
I want to believe in what he was seeking
I want to believe that he is still swimming
toward that aina for which he feels
that word which is so hard to say

I want to believe in the word
But Brother George doesn't say it
He doesn't sing it in his smooth falsetto
in the melodies of aloha aina
There is no chance of seeing him walk up to the stage
pick up his guitar and smile the word at you across the room
The tourists, they twist their malihini tongues
The tour guides mouth it with smog-filled lungs
Politicians keep taking it out, dusting off the carcass
of a once-proud 3 syllable guaranteed vote-getter
You find its ghosts on dump trucks, magazines
airplanes, rent-a-cars
anywhere they want the dollar
They can sell you anything with aloha and a smile
even pineapples that came here from
(you guessed it) America!
They'll sell you too, servants of the USA
And if you don't believe they have the nerve
think of the ocean
They put up signs as close as they dare
And when his spirit comes back to land
the first thing he'll see is a big sign with that word
painted on, carved in, flashing with electricity
That word, so hard to say

I was going to believe that word
I was going to believe all those corporations
that seemed to spring up like mushrooms after a light rain
I was going to believe when they divided up
the home-land of a living people
and called it real estate   or 50th state
or   Aloha State
I was going to believe we would still be able
to go up to the mountains, out to the country beaches
to the ocean where waves wash the islands
the islands which remind us we've all traveled a long way to
get here

We all wanted a garden of our own in the world
We believed we'd all have peace
(and a piece of the aloha and of the state if we worked for it)
We're all pursuing the same dream!
So many of us are trying to get to the mountains, the beaches
so many trying to swim in the waves
legs kicking, arms paddling like the arms
of George Helm stroking towards a familiar beach
which he respected and belonged to by birth
for which he felt something no word can express
except for that word which is hard to say
unless we all live it!

I want to live the word "aloha"
But the body of George Helm is lost at sea
the practice continues on Kahoolawe
the buildings follow the roads
the roads carry thousands of cars filled with people
following their dreams of Hawaii or Paradise
to Waikiki where girls sell their hips
singers sell their voices
the island which has been sold is lit up all night
while the king with outstretched hand
has forgotten how to use his spear
George Helm is dead
and that word is not forgotten
It rings in my ears every day
I want us to live the word "aloha"
but it's so hard just to say

House Bill 1129 was a bill for an act making an appropriation for archaeological and historical research on the island of Kahoolawe. It did not pass.

60 PKO Testimony in support of House Bill 1129

George Helm, Loretta A. Ritte

Testimony re: House Bill 1129
House Committee on Culture and Arts
February 25, 1977

Mr. Chairman and members of the committee:

Whereas, on May 15, 1971 the President of the United States, the Honorable Richard Nixon, applied to the National Historic Preservation Act an Executive Order (#11593) which required the heads of federal agencies, which included the Navy, to co-operate with the Secretary of Interior to locate, inventory, and nominate all sites and areas that may appear to qualify for listing on the Federal Registry; and

Whereas, the State of Hawaii's Historic Preservation Office, as indicated in the Summary of Findings of February 10, 1977, spent 26 days on Kaho'olawe surveying 4,100 acres which amounts to only 14% of the island's total acreage, and has thus far recorded 30 archaeological sites which all except one are eligible for the National Register of Historic Places; and

Whereas, the island of Kaho'olawe is under the control of the Department of the Navy pursuant to Executive Order 10436; and

Whereas, it is the responsibility of the Navy pursuant to Executive Order 11593 to initiate the process of locating and nominating all historical sites and locations on the island of Kaho'olawe; and

Whereas, it is known that the State of Hawaii and the Department of the Navy are *jointly* surveying the island of Kaho'olawe absent a proper *cost factor* determination based on their respective responsibilities; and

Whereas, it is known that the Navy continues to bomb Kaho'olawe which could have negative effects on the historic sites needing surveying; and

Whereas it is believed that the State's archaeological survey team need better means to implement a proper survey, in fairness to the Native Hawaiians, rightful heirs to the culture being surveyed; and

Therefore be it resolved that the PKO supports House Bill 1129.

Telegram to President Carter—February 2, 1977

DEAR MR. PRESIDENT

UNITED STATES NAVY HAS SUSPENDED BOMBING OF TARGET ISLAND OF KAHO'OLAWE HERE IN HAWAII BECAUSE OF OUR INVASION. TWO NATIVE HAWAIIANS WALTER RITTE AND RICHARD SAWYER REMAIN ON THIS ISLAND SACRED TO

US HAWAIIANS AND WILL CONTINUE TO OCCUPY IT UNTIL BOMBING OF OUR HEIAUS (SHRINES) AND DESTRUCTION OF OUR CULTURE IS PERMANENTLY STOPPED.

AS PRESIDENT YOU HAVE AUTHORITY TO RESCIND EXECUTIVE ORDER 10436 ALLOWING BOMBING. AS NATIVE HAWAIIANS WE INVADED KAHO'OLAWE TO PROTEST THIS DESECRATION. WE HAVE

VOLUNTARILY RETURNED TO HONOLULU TO TELL THE WORLD OF THE SACRED NATURE OF THE ISLAND AND TO CONVEY THE DETERMINATION OF RITTE AND SAWYER TO REMAIN ON KAHO'OLAWE. OTHER HAWAIIANS ARE NOW PREPARING TO JOIN THEM IN THIS INVASION.

WE NATIVE HAWAIIANS WANT YOU TO HEAR OUR VOICES.

CONTINUOUS DISREGARD OF OUR SERIOUS INTENTION HAS FORCED US TO TAKE THIS ACTION. WE ASK TO MEET WITH YOU PERSONALLY TO DISCUSS THIS INCREASINGLY CRITICAL SITUATION, ALONG WITH CONGRESSMAN DANIEL AKAKA THE COUNCIL OF HAWAIIAN ORGANIZATIONS AND THE PROTECT KAHO'OLAWE OHANA. WE AWAIT YOUR RESPONSE AT PHONE

NUMBER 808 841-5961. WE CANNOT OVERSTATE THE SERIOUSNESS OF THIS SITUATION.

WITH RESPECT
GEORGE HELM
FRANCIS KA'UHANE
CHARLES WARRINGTON

Jill Harwood. Grade 5

Kahoolawe now is
an island of Perish all
the Hawaiians want it back!
The Navy needs it for bombing.
The argument stills stands at
the White House.

"We are not criminals, and our conviction and belief is to protect and perpetuate the righteousness of the land."

Letter to President Carter

February 16, 1977

The President
The White House
Washington, D.C. 20500

Dear Mr. President:

We are native Hawaiians here in Washington, D.C., not to waste anyone's valuable time, nor do we want any one of you to waste our time. However, our presence here is as a result of governmental negligence and lack of response to our "plea." We received no response from you even after a telegram was sent to your office from Hawaii on February 2, 1977, requesting to meet with you or any White House member personally. The matter—which is an executive one and not a congressional one—is one of emergency and we ask assistance from the White House to prevent a possible "Wounded Knee" and to look seriously into the souls of our Hawaiian people.

We both have been arrested, along with three others, and are awaiting trial for trespassing on an island considered to be very sacred to Hawaiians; yet it is, by Executive Order, a military reservation used specifically since 1941 by the Department of the Navy as a bombing target and though only a portion is being bombed, the entire island is endangered environmentally and ecologically by Man's lack of concern. The island is 45 square miles, potent with life—it is not a barren rock and the barrenness is in those souls that see it as such. We saw, after walking the entire island, miles of unnecessary erosion—just miles of hard ground with single trees and patches of grass, here and there.

We are not criminals, and our conviction and belief is to protect and perpetuate the righteousness of our land. The real crime is to destroy the life of land and life of Man. Two other native Hawaiians remain hidden on the island to speak loudly their serious concern—yet the Navy continues to drop bombs on the island regardless of the fact that the *possibility* of injuring and taking away life exists. Regardless of the discoveries by the State's archaeological and historical survey team that prove the island's historical treasures and value, the desecration continues. Regardless of the fact that Hawaiians know of a population of farm people once living on the island, the Navy sees the land as useless. The tradition of our people has been taken away by progress and money interest and continues to be so as there is neglect. We are a dying race, an endangered species, and we cannot allow further injury to an already wounded soul.

We have vowed to protect the remnants of our culture at whatever cost, and the culture cannot exist without the land. What is essential to know is that we are dealing with National Security and the interest of the people. Only one Congressman turned his ears to us, because he is a native Hawaiian and he understands the language. We come before you not to lay any useless rhetoric on you, but to have you see the seriousness of the matter. It is your duty, Mr. President, to listen to the plea of a neglected people.

We are native Americans too. What must we do to hear from you?

Aloha,
PROTECT KAHOOLAWE OHANA

George Helm
Francis Ka'uhane

Tracy Lani Delatori. Grade 5

Kahoolawe once was a foreign island.
It had some foreign men and one Hawaiian man. He was the strongest guy on that island. One day he got into a fight with the foreign man. So the Hawaiian guy said to the foreign man, "I warning you. If you no leave me alone, I going beat you up. So watch it."

On February 11, 1977, George Helm was asked to speak before the state House of Representatives. It was an unprecedented event. No non-member had ever been allowed to address the House before. Helm declared it "a step forward in helping to bridge the gap between the politicians and the people who elect you here."

Steve Shrader

George Helm in action at the State Capitol. The voice and soul of the body politic.

Steve Shrader

Speech to the State House

George Helm

February 11, 1977

Mahalo nui. Thank you for this opportunity. Forgive me while I need time to gather my thoughts. The privilege to speak to you folks comes about by invitation. I was invited to here to speak by Mr. Peters and Mr. Yuen.

Yesterday, after the arraignment of two of the trespassers arrested on Kahoolawe, the ʻOhana who supported the movement marched to the rotunda here and we prayed and made statements to the media and said, "Akua kokua Walter Ritte and Richard Sawyer whose lives are endangered by the possibility of bombs." But moreso by the negligence of the politicians. If God can hear us, why cannot the politicians. That was the statement we made. That's all. I was walking away from the Capitol; I had nothing to say and I was asked to come here and I came. Mr. Peters asked me if I wanted to speak, or I was told that I could speak. I don't know; there was some confusion. When I found out I couldn't, I was ready to leave so I could do my work—I have plenty of work outside of this arena. So he said, "If there is anything I can do to speak for you," so I said, "Well, we're coming up with a court order at two o'clock in Sam King's court to come up with a temporary restraining order and I only want is some reaction from the politicians." Somebody, I don't know who. I am not going to point finger to no one, and I want somebody to intervene. We are arrested for trespassing and we are considered criminals.

We are motivated to pursue the action of protecting whatever is left of our culture and very basically, it is simple. The culture exists only if the life of the land is perpetuated in righteousness; that belongs to my ancestors. You folks are using this to get paid, to build your homes, to give your kids an education, to bring kids over here and listen to you give a

Steve Shrader

political rhetoric. I came here to ask; to help some people's lives, and I am talking about possibility or probability and the science of mathematics help us guys figure out the odds and averages. Regardless of that fact, we are supposed to respond with a sensitivity to this emergency and we had no response from anybody except Mr. Peters, Mr. Yuen, Kinau Kamalii, Dan Akaka.

Our organization is one year old and sitting in an office for a long time, I am sure everybody behind the powers of the political pedestal know my name. I come just to support the resolution and very grateful for having this opportunity upon invitation. This is a step forward in helping to bridge the gap between the politicians and the people who elect you here.

The bombs over there, for me, is not the danger; it's the negligence. For one year, my commitment is to Walter Ritte, Richard Sawyer and their wives who are on that aina, to make a meeting with the President of the United States, with Congressman Akaka and the Council of Hawaiian Organizations, and I would put my life out for that meeting and six other people have done so. A potential lawyer has given his sacrifice. He could have been convicted for felony. The social worker could have lost his job and you should listen to what I have to say because you are being paid. We never had a chance to talk. This is the first time something like this is happening—you guys are going to hear it. Please kokua; do something—some reaction. Every county made a resolution—County of Hawaii—every county did. Bills have been passed and when something like this is happening, nothing is being done. All I'm asking for is a reaction, positive or negative, but please support us if you can, and we are talking about Aloha 'Aina 'Ohana and if you cannot understand it, go do your homework.

Mahalo.

"We are talking about Aloha 'Aina 'Ohana, and if you cannot understand it, go do your homework."

Steve Shrader

George's Diary: Fourth Occupation of Kaho'olawe, Jan. 1977

Last Sunday of the month

Day of Kaho'olawe occupation—using flashlight to write this note—

Much has been done in preparation for this protest (spiritually especially). Without the spiritual element, life would be like an empty breath, no substance.

Pi'ilani is guiding us through this adventure as we offered ho'okupu and mohai aloha to the kupuna of the past at Hale o Pi'ilani.

The occupation of the military reservation is not so much a defiance as it is a responsibility to express our legitimate concern for the land of the Hawaiian. Kaho'olawe is a part of my culture—no other person but a Hawaiian can understand the pains of a lost culture. We are against warfare but more so against imperialism. Imperialism suffocates the growth of individual ethnicity.

Walter and I: We spent some moments on searching for pohaku. With the best use of our senses we tried to detect the pohaku that radiated a strangeness, different characteristics from other rocks. Only a sensitive human being who has not been robbed of his individual soul by mass education will understand us, Hawaiians looking at pohaku for the lost world.

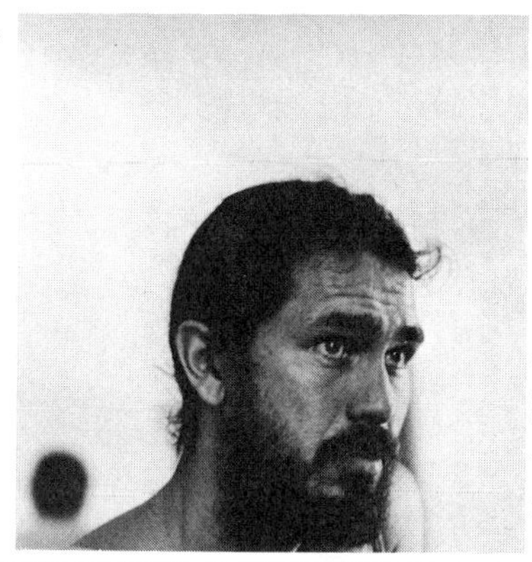

Alexis Higdon

George Helm— A True Hawaiian

Walter Ritte, Jr.

It was his heart that made him stand above the rest, his love affairs with women that tore him apart, as he could not bear to hurt any of them. His love for these islands made him commit his life to protecting the land. He would cry in sadness when he was unable to explain to the military the concept of *Aloha Aina.* It was his heart that allowed him to give all of himself to *aloha aina.* It was his heart that brought thousands of people to love him.

It was his smile that melted away all fear of an "activist" who was about to speak. When the words started to flow, you knew you were listening to a well educated man who demanded *we all do our "homework."*

It was his mind that put him into hours of deep thought, hours in libraries, museums, genealogies, and quiet places. It was his mind that drove him from island to island in search of the knowledge from our *kupuna.*

It was his music which created a neutral space for all to come close to the man, *George Helm.* It was his music which allowed him to caress his culture. It was his music which allowed us to observe *a true Hawaiian.*

It was the combination of all his talents, finely interwoven, that made him a complicated spiritual man who was driven by a thirst for Hawaiian spiritualism and *mana.* Day after day, *kupuna* after *kupuna* gave George the knowledge and *mana* to change from the "nice" Hawaiian to the "activist" Hawaiian who loved so dearly.

"Far worse than man not having land is man not having identity, aspects of culture, pride and self-esteem, dignity."

Advertiser photo by Edwin Tanji (courtesy HNL ADV)

George Jarrett Helm, Jr.

Kimo had all the positive qualities George Helm had wished for in all young Hawaiians: he had pride in his culture—and no sense of inferiority—a good education, a sense of purpose, and a willingness to give of himself.

reprint by Ed Greevy

James Kimo Mitchell

Kimo Mitchell—A Life

Rodney Morales

James Kimo Mitchell was born on February 15, 1952, in Keanae, Maui, a taro-growing community along the rugged, winding road to Hana. Kimo was the youngest of the five children of Harry, Sr., and Pearl Mitchell. Like just about everyone else in this Hawaiian community, Kimo grew up practicing *aloha 'aina:* along with family members he learned to cultivate taro and lilikoi, and fish for po'opaa and akule. Kimo's father, known as Uncle Harry, likes to say that the ocean was their icebox and the land their grocery store.

Kimo grew up fast. Always big for his age, he liked to challenge his older brother Harry, Jr. (whom he had outgrown) to wrestling matches. He would try to overpower him but he never succeeded, for Harry practiced Kung Fu.

Swimming came naturally to Kimo. The ocean was practically the back door of the Mitchell's home. His father says he "could swim the channel four, five times, like one turtle. Nobody could keep up with him. I told the mother, 'The ocean goin' take him.'"

When he was twelve, Kimo was given the opportunity to spend his summer vacation fishing for salmon in Alaska. Dick Avey, a teacher at Keanae School, had arranged this work/vacation for students who wanted to earn their keep as fishermen. It was not play, but hard work, and Kimo adjusted to it well.

After attending Keanae School, Kimo went to St. Anthony's, then Baldwin High School in Wailuku. There he played linebacker for the Baldwin High School team that won the Maui Championship in his senior year. In the game that signalled the end of Lahainaluna High School's long reign as Maui champions, the *Maui News* reported: "Richie Nakashima and James Mitchell spearheaded the blitzing defense that had the Luna's quarterback, Gerald Lau Hee, scrambling and rushing his passes all night." At the end of his season with the Baldwin Bears, Kimo and his blitzing cohort Richie were cited

Photo courtesy of Mitchell family

as the two members of the Maui All-Star team who deserved special mention. (The trophies he received were added to the trophy collection that sits to this day on his old dresser in his father's Keanae home.)

After graduating with the Baldwin class of 1970, Kimo passed up a chance to attend the University of Hawaii and opted instead for mainland colleges. First he attended Coalinga Junior College in California, then he transferred to Fresno State. At both schools he played football and in his senior year at Fresno State he received All-Conference honors. Kimo also received feelers from the Chicago Bears of the National Football League but took his father's suggestion that he not try out. "You only going against hills now," Uncle Harry said, "In the NFL you gotta face mountains."

Kimo's mind was not only on football and the girls that his muscular good looks attracted. He spent much of his time in serious study toward a Bachelor of Science degree in Natural Resources and Criminology.

He was the pride and joy of his family and meant everything to his mother. Whenever Kimo came home from college during a break, his mother would be waiting—at the airport, even—with poi and raw fish. Then the family would go out for a Chinese dinner.

The last time Kimo came home from college everything was different. No fish and poi at the airport. No Chinese dinner. No graduation party either, though his mother had insisted. Kimo didn't want one; he didn't feel like celebrating anything. His mother had been stricken with cancer and was in the hospital receiving treatment.

Pearl Mitchell died soon after that. Kimo's sister, Sara Jean, came from California for the funeral. His other sister, Isabel, who was pregnant at the time, remained in Germany, where her husband was stationed. After the funeral, Sara Jean went back to her home in Downey, California. Isabel eventually settled in California also, near Fort Ord. Since Pearl—named after her mother—was the only sister left at Keanae, she took on

James Kimo Mitchell, Baldwin High School student.

Photo courtesy of Mitchell family

her mother's role. She washed clothes and cooked meals for Kimo.

But there was little else her brother needed. His summer in Alaska and his years in college had made him very independent. And the solid support his family had always provided had given him a strong sense of self-esteem. (In fact, Kimo had all the positive qualities George Helm had wished for in all young Hawaiians: he had pride in his culture—and no sense of inferiority—a good education, a sense of purpose, and a willingness to give of himself. Helm would say he had plenty of *mana.*)

Like many young men his age, Kimo lived as fast a life as one could in the slow-moving town of Hana. He often sped to and from work, making the hour-and-a-half drive in forty-five minutes. "If we saw a red thing passing through the town," friends say, "that was Kimo." Later on, when Kimo bought a VW rabbit, "We used to see this green thing..."

Kimo smashed up his car one day, after having a few drinks at the home of the Lind family, good friends of his. When Hana police brought him home, Kimo told his father, "Only da car sore." His father told the police to lock him up. Kimo said, "The bridge wen' move on da road." His father then said, "You oughta go in movies, you one clown." Of course he wasn't arrested; Hana is a small community, and everyone knows everyone else, even the cops.

Enjoy, enjoy. That seemed to be Kimo's motto. He enjoyed playing the ukulele and wrote the words for the song, "Seven Pools," which his father set to music. He paddled outrigger canoe for the Hana Canoe Club senior men's team. He also spent hours hunting with friends in the mountains above the town. (Hunting was new to him, they recall, but he took to it as well as every other sport.)

And he did some commercial fishing. He and friend Sluggo Hahn got together and bought a boat for that purpose. (Once Kimo took his father and brother on a fishing trip. They caught about a dozen fish. Kimo divided them up this way: one for his father, one for Harry, Jr., and ten for himself. They

Photo courtesy of Mitchell family

Kimo, clowning around with brother Harry Jr.

looked at him questioningly. "Gotta pay fo' da boat, eh?" was Kimo's smiling reply.

Kimo Mitchell met George Helm in 1976. Though he did not get to know George well until later on, Kimo knew of him. George's mother's family, the Kokos, were from Hana, and George seemed to be related to everyone from Keanae to Kipahulu. (Kimo and George were actually distant cousins.)

Though the leaders of many organizations came to the Hana area to talk about local issues, George Helm stood out. Unlike so many political types, George spoke with humility and at a grassroots level. Hana people felt as if a son had returned. George genuinely cared and worked hard to help the community in its struggle to preserve its Hawaiian identity and culture, and to maintain its access to land and water. And besides, he played guitar and sang as if it were fifty years ago (at least that's what the old folks said).

At about this time, Kimo began to be concerned about the welfare of the community that had given him so much. He became involved in local organizations, doing whatever he could for the *keiki o ka aina* (children of the land). He emerged as a leader, not the sort who spoke in front of crowds but, according to friend John Lind, an "on-the-side kind of leader." Kimo related best to people in one-to-one situations, and because he spoke "good English" when he had to or chose to, the others wanted him to speak for them.

Kimo began thinking of going back to school. He wanted to get another degree, this time in education. There was no organized sports in Hana, and Kimo thought he could help the children of the town by starting a program and working actively as coach.

But fate intervened. Because Kimo and Sluggo had a boat, and because George Helm and other Protect Kahoolawe Ohana members "felt really good about the Hana boys," by January

1977 Kimo and Sluggo were providing transportation to and from Kahoolawe. When Helm went to Hana to ask for help, Kimo quickly said yes, largely because he "felt good about George."

So on January 30, 1977, Kimo and Sluggo dropped off Helm, Ritte, Richard Sawyer, and two others on the "target island." Ritte and Sawyer were to stay on the island in protest of the bombing and had brought enough food and water for two weeks. The others were to let themselves be arrested and removed to Honolulu.

Three weeks later, on February 20, Kimo and Sluggo attempted to return to resupply Ritte and Sawyer but were foiled by a Coast Guard Helicopter. (The Coast Guard, by then, had at least four boats and two helicopters in the area to prevent boats from landing. People had also been "sneaking" over on surfboards or swimming to and from the island for the past few weeks. No one knew for sure how many people were on the island at any one time.)

From then until early March, Kimo and his friends had little to do with the heavy activity around Kahoolawe, and they maintained their low profile back in Hana. Then on Friday, March 4, while Kimo was working in his father's taro patch, he was surprised to see George Helm approaching with several others. Helm told Kimo and the other Hana boys who had gathered at the Mitchell home that he needed their kokua. He said he had to get Ritte and Sawyer off the island; he feared they were in danger. (This danger, he said, had been foretold in his dreams and in the dreams of others. There had also been signs, particularly a ring around the moon.) They knew George was sincere and they replied, "Shoot, we go."

Helm also said that he needed to take someone with him to the island who was good in the water. Kimo, the excellent waterman, volunteered. Then they all went to the back of the Mitchell home to *pule*, pray, and prepare to leave.

As they were getting into the car, Kimo's brother, Harry, came by. He told Kimo, "Hey brother, you're not going, huh?" Kimo seemed torn, hesitant, but then expressed that he was going. They seemed to be in a rush and didn't have time to talk, so Harry just said, "Take it easy." He never saw his brother again.

The group drove down to Hasegawa General Store, purchased the supplies they needed—waterproof flashlights, batteries, canned goods—and headed toward Kipahulu. Mishaps abounded. At "Make Man's Bridge," the right rear wheel of the trailer hauling the boat slipped off and the axle broke. They checked the damage and quickly decided a generator and welding equipment would be needed, as well as a forklift to raise the boat. Because the bridge was blocked, cars began to back up along the Hana road. People gathered around to watch.

After the seemingly impossible task was finished, a slow-moving procession of cars headed toward Nuu Bay. It looked like a parade. Everyone seemed to know what was going on. (In Hana, news travels fast.)

Spirits were high, but when the group reached the bay they saw that the waves were kicking up. Launching the boat was extremely difficult. Several onlookers finally jumped into the rough surf and pushed it into the channel so that the motor could be started. A little later, off the coast of Kaupo, the fuel line became disconnected and the boat was pushed dangerously close to the rocky coast by the high surf. Luckily, the line was quickly fixed; it was smooth sailing after that. Thinking that their troubles were over, the group headed toward Kihei for a short rest and some final planning.

At about two a.m. the next morning, a Saturday, they headed toward Kahoolawe. Billy Mitchell (no relation to Kimo) had joined them in Kihei as planned. Helm had picked him to go to the island because, like Kimo, he was an excellent waterman. As they neared the island, they saw what seemed to be a Coast Guard helicopter approaching from a distance. Someone said "Hit it" and Kimo Mitchell, George Helm, and Billy Mitchell jumped into the water with their two surfboards, an inner tube, and their supplies, carefully wrapped in plastic bags.

Kimo, rt., posing with other National Parks Service Rangers.

Photo courtesy of Mitchell family

According to the people left on the boat, pickups had been scheduled for five a.m. that same morning and—largely to avoid the Coast Guard—eleven that night. When the boat approached the island for the first pickup, two men waved them off and the crew returned to Kihei. They never made the eleven o'clock pickup. Kimo and Sluggo's boat—its three plugs unscrewed—had sunk at the pier off Kihei. Efforts to get another boat went on for two days. By the time they found another boat, Billy Mitchell had been picked up by a Coast Guard helicopter. While being shuttled to Honolulu, he announced that Kimo Mitchell and George Helm were missing at sea. He told of the attempt by the three to make it back to Maui on the two surboards they had brought with them. He said that Helm had cut his forehead while trying to enter the high surf. When he last saw them, he said, they were struggling in the rough waves near Molokini, a tiny, crescent-shaped island about two miles off Maui's coastline. Billy Mitchell left them and returned to Kahoolawe to get help. He walked the island for a day and finally stumbled upon a military camp and gave himself up. Search efforts, which went on for over two weeks, turned up no trace of Mitchell or Helm, and—except for the inner tube, a t-shirt and a pair of tabis that belonged to Kimo—no trace of their supplies.

Everyone who knew Kimo Mitchell feels that he stayed with Helm till the very end, no matter what happened out at sea. That was Kimo. His sister-in-law, Joanne Mitchell, says, "He would help anybody. He was the type who would help the friend of a friend of a friend..." He was generous to a fault.

Soon after Kimo disappeared, his NAUI diver's certificate arrived at his Keanae home. It certified him as a classified water specialist with a WSI (Water Safety Instruction) II rating. "Always down the beach," his father says. "That's where you find him." Later, Uncle Harry says in an uncharacteristically subdued tone: "He had a short life. But at least he had a life."

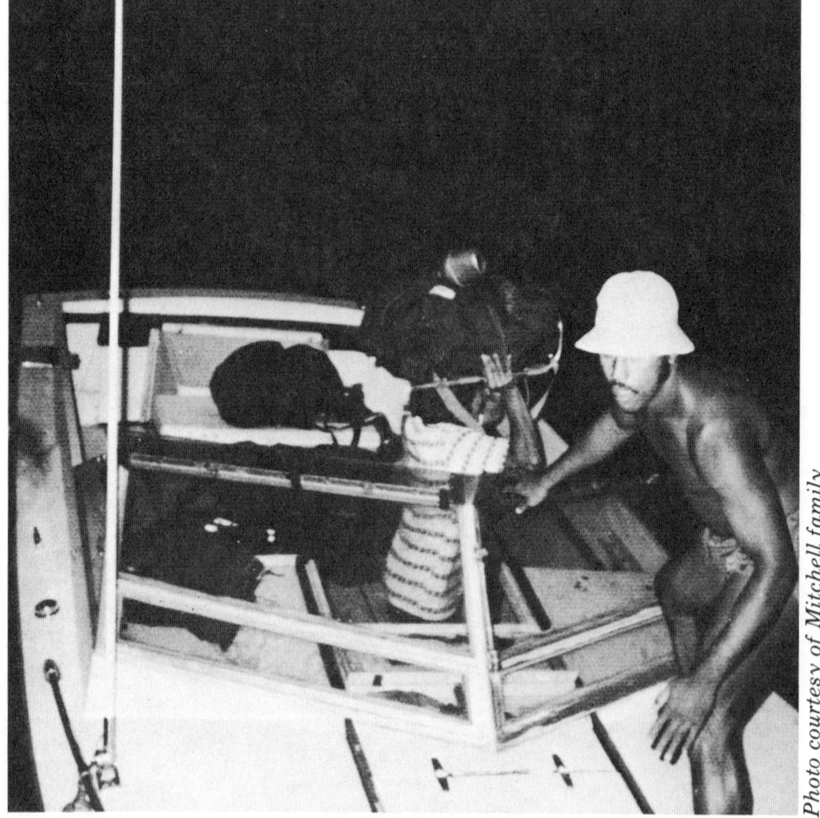

Photo courtesy of Mitchell family

Kimo and Sluggo Hahn unloading the boat for January 30, 1977 illegal landing. Last picture taken of Kimo.

Kimo, with father,
"Uncle Harry" Mitchell

Photo courtesy of Mitchell family

Seven Pools

Words by James Kimo Mitchell
Music by Harry Kunihi Mitchell

This side of Heaven drenched in the dew
Peaceful and cool
Seven Pools in Kipahulu

You are the symbol of loveliness
within my heart
Your splendid beauty will never fade

Wet in gentle rains from the mountains
to the sea
Keep you beautiful throughout the year

Fragrance of flowers fills the air
along the way
You are the answer to my only dream

God's world is my world
at Seven Pools in Kipahulu
Till we meet again, aloha, I love you

Mele o Kahoolawe

Harry Kunihi Mitchell

Aloha ku'u moku
O Kaho'olawe
Mai kinohi kou inoa

O Kanaloa

Kohemalamalama

Lau kanaka 'ole

Hiki mai na pua

E ho'omalu mai

Alu like kakou
Lahui Hawai'i
Mai ka la hiki mai
I ka la kau a'e
Ku pa'a a hahai
Hoikaika na kanaka
Kau li'i makou
Nui ke aloha no ka 'aina

Hanohano na pua
O Hawai'i nei
No ke kaua kauholo

Me ka aupuni
Pa'a pu ka mana'o
No ka pono o ka 'aina

Imua na pua
Lanakila Kaho'olawe

Song of Kahoolawe

Harry Kunihi Mitchell

Love my island
Kaho'olawe
From the Beginning your
name
was Kanaloa
You are the Southern
beacon
Barren and without
population
Until you were invaded by
nine young men
And they granted you
peace

Let us band together
the Hawaiian Kingdom
from sun up
to sun down
Stand together and follow
Be strong young people
We are but a few in number
but our love for the land
is unlimited

Popular is the young people
of Hawaii nei
For the civil strife they
caused
against the government
together in one thought
to bring prosperity to the
land
Forward young people
and bring salvation to
Kaho'olawe

Kahoolawe,
poor island of Hawaii,
it must be painful
when all those big bombs hit.
Unfortunately they don't miss.

Keith Karlo. Grade 5

Kahoolawe
    is a rocky hill
        with bombs on it.

Ann Kawabata. Grade 5

Kahoolawe I love you
Kahoolawe say you love me too
I've only seen you from a distance
I wish I could see you up close.

Robin Bodinus. Grade 5

Kahoolawe once was an island that people could go on. They could live on it. Until America came. It is a bombing place now. I wonder if people can go there like before? If they could I would sail on it. I would fly to it. I would walk to it. Even if I get tired.

Elmo Savella. Grade 5

Kahoolawe was once a Hawaiian Island where the people of old Hawaii worshipped their Gods and it was a very Secret Island. And they say it's so secret that if someone went there they would get bad luck for the rest of their lives because they were trespassing on the forbidden zone of old Hawaii. Or that person would be sentenced to death! If they got away that was the last of their good luck.

Kahoolawe now is a bombing area for the Navy but still they might get back luck because the Heiaus are still standing.

Lori Zimmerman. Grade 4

Star-Bulletin photo

Kaulua

Kimo Mitchell was a tall Hawaiian, and like most big men he has a big heart. The first and last time I saw Kimo he was at the same church hall where George spoke in Hawaiian to the people. We were having a village luau and it was b.y.o.b. but I didn't know it. Kimo, seeing me suffer, handed me his only bottle of beer.His smile was so warm, his aloha so pure, he was so happy that he had something to give someone that made them happy.... he never thought about going without himself. Kimo's head is very mellow and kind. He could be kind because he knew his strength. Kimo is the embodiment of the aloha spirit. There isn't a mean bone in his body... He asked for a chance in his lifetime to work the aina like his father and grandfather and his ancestors.

R. Morales

Moeʻuhane

Joseph Balaz

I dream of
the ways of the past—

I cannot go back.

I hike the hills
    and valleys of Wahiawa,
walking through crystal
        streams
    and scaling green cliffs

I play in the waves
        of Waimea,
and spear fish
    from the reefs of Kawailoa.

I grow bananas, ʻulu,
        and papayas,
    in the way of the ʻaina.

I cannot go back—

I never left.

Kahoolawe—the barren island that gave birth to a resurgence of aloha aina.

Alexis Higdon

Aloha ʻAina

Kalani Meinecke

Aloha ʻAina. Love for the Land. The Native Hawaiians' deep and enduring love for their *ʻaina,* land, is manifest in the entirety of their being—in their philosophy of life, in their religion, in the fascination with places and place names, and in their brilliant musical heritage.

Literally thousands of Hawaiian songs exist which extoll the overwhelming presence and beauty of nature, and its powerful effect upon human affairs. So close is the association of man with land that the basic terms of human kinship identification spring from the land and the plants grown in the soil. The basic Hawaiian family unit is called the *ʻohana,* a term derived from *ʻoha,* root offshoot of the parent taro plant. The terms for alternate generations, *kupuna,* grandparent (as well as ancestor), and *moʻopuna,* grandchild (as well as descendant), echo the term *puna,* spring of life-giving water, a term symbolizing the assurance of human continuity and life itself.

From Kaʻu to Kaʻula, from Kauaʻi to Kahoʻolawe, the Hawaiian soul continues to pledge its allegiance to the beauty and the integrity of the life-sustaining *ʻaina.*

Kahoolawe. The "water-hole" was created by a mock atomic blast in the late 1950s.

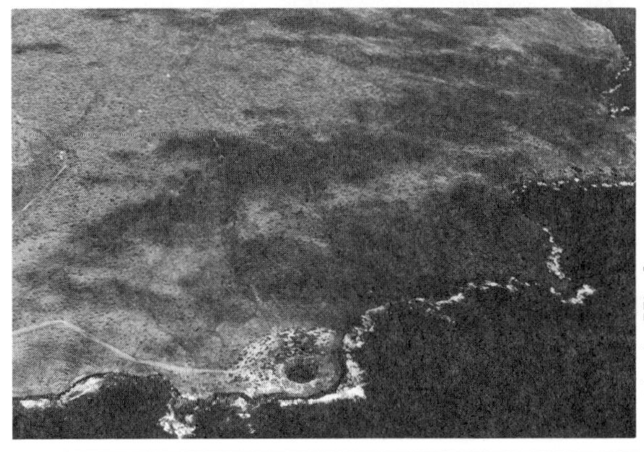

Alexis Higdon

Aloha ʻAina

Protect Kahoʻolawe ʻOhana

This is the calling of our Kupuna . . .
Creation, not desecration
Proper use, not gross-misuse
Respect of land, not abuse of land
Self-sufficiency, not false dependency
Living heritage, not a museum heritage
A Puʻu-Honua, not an off-limits area
Caretakers, not owners of this ʻAina Hawaiʻi
Take only what you need for today, not take all and sell
And to reach into our past to learn the many other
values which sustained over three hundred thousand
Hawaiʻi people in harmony with nature.

Kahoolawe once was a beautiful island
where a valley was filled with beautiful palm
trees swaying and birds singing songs and
a beautiful waterfall flowing gently upon the rocks.
Kahoolawe now is a target island for bombing.

Jacky Maile Kaanana. Grade 5

Kahoolawe once was
nice land. But people came
to ruin and that's what
they did. They ruined
our native land.

Arianna Altfeld. Grade 4

Kahoolawe once was a giant.
The people living on this giant
had to feed him. He grew lots
of food on his body. The
people began running out of
food so they asked their god
how to get rid of him. He said
they had to sing to him. They
sang to him everyday, but
nothing happened. Then a little
girl sang to him. She sang so
beautifully, he turned into an
Island, Kahoolawe.

Andy Pele. Grade 5

Kahoolawe is an island for
bombing, bombing, bombing.

Kahoolawe is an island for
death, death, death.

Samuel Waiohu. Grade 4

Fire rescue and other volunteers mapping out search strategy.

Alexis Higdon

Map 1—The Search

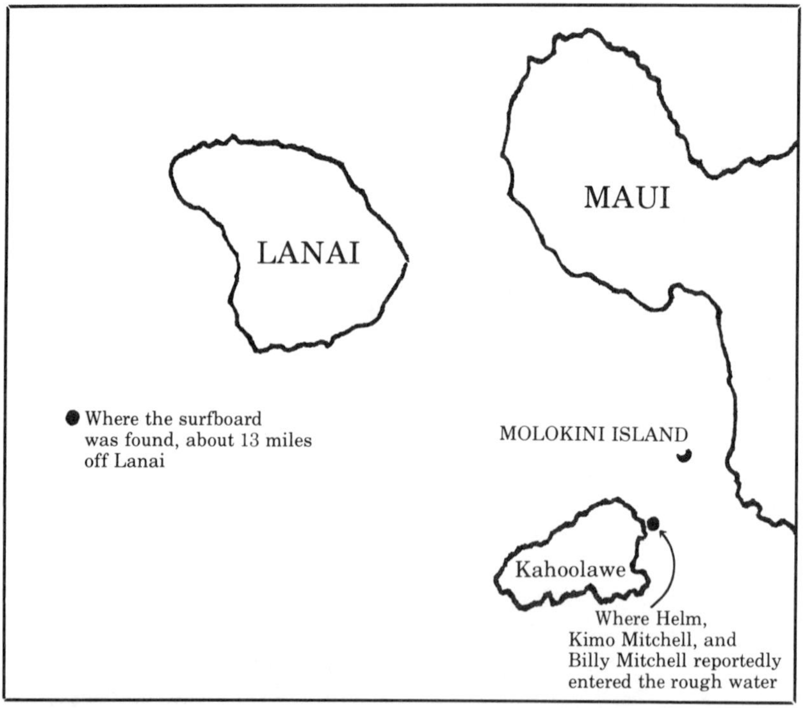

LANAI

MAUI

MOLOKINI ISLAND

Kahoolawe

● Where the surfboard was found, about 13 miles off Lanai

Where Helm, Kimo Mitchell, and Billy Mitchell reportedly entered the rough water

On March 8, 1977, Billy Mitchell reported that his two companions, George Helm and Kimo Mitchell, were missing at sea. The following day, a massive search was launched that involved military personnel, fire rescue specialists, family and friends of the two, and other volunteers. The surfboard that the missing two reportedly shared was found about 13 miles off the island of Lanai.

Alexis Higdon

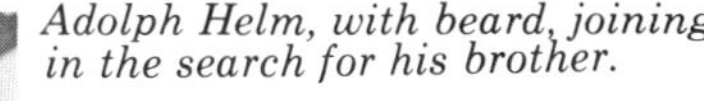

Adolph Helm, with beard, joining in the search for his brother.

R. Morales

The surfboard. Billy Mitchell says he last saw Helm and Mitchell on this surfboard, struggling in the waves off Molokini Island.

Map 2—Maui and Kahoolawe

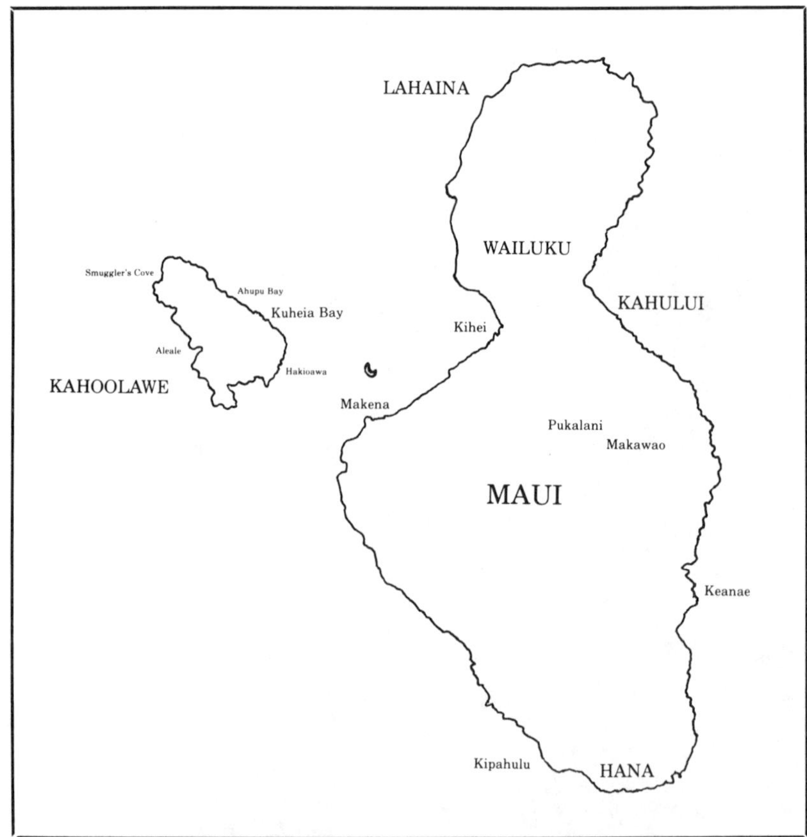

Maui is seen both in legend and in shape as being a maternal figure. Kahoolawe's fetus shape enhances the sense of mother-child relationship between the two islands. Some say also that Molokini island, where Helm and Mitchell were reportedly last seen, is the umbilical cord, cut and dried out.

While Maui, the nurturing mother, flourishes, Kahoolawe, the cut-off child, is deprived of nourishment. Its shape, therefore, within the context of the other islands, only enhances the sorry fate of the island.

Map 3—Kahoolawe

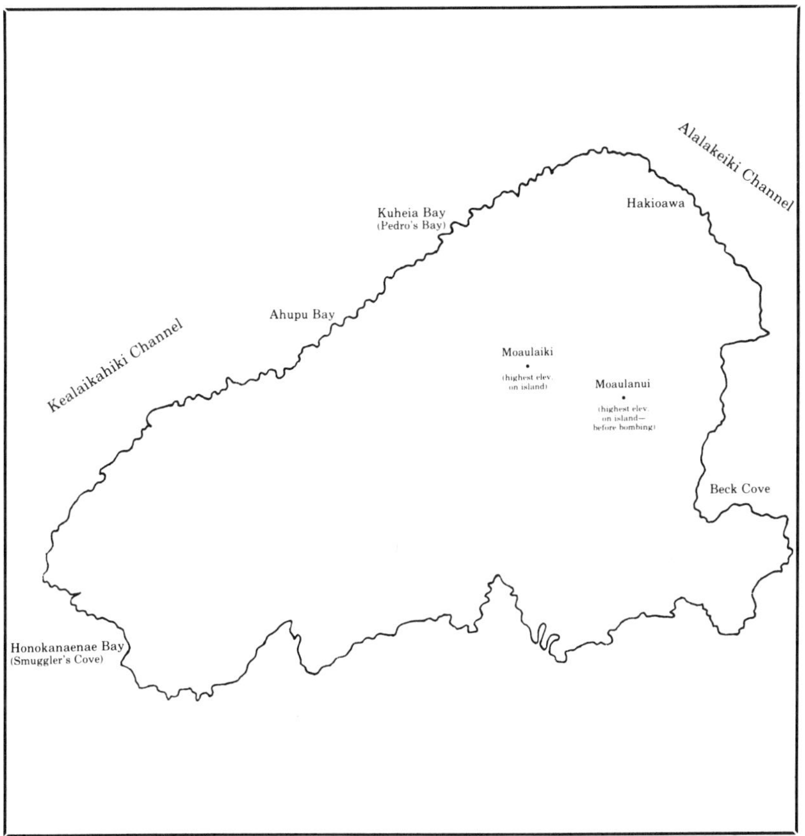

Alexis Higdon

Alexis Higdon

Malamalama, or blessing ceremonies using bonfires, were held on March 23, 1977—George Helm's 27th birthday—throughout the Hawaiian Islands.

Death At Sea

Concrete Poem by Richard Hamasaki
Serigraph by Mark Hamasaki

Poem for Kahoolawe

Kahoolawe is quiet
as the sun on it
as the wind whispers
to the island
well you rest you
think

Tammy Laborte. Grade 4

Kahoolawe is now the place
to bomb Hawaiians

Allen Darisay. Grade 4

The "Eddie" in verse 2 refers to Eddie Aikau, another Hawaiian lost at sea during the Hokulea's *ill-fated 1978 voyage.*

Where Does It All Lead To (1978)

words and music by Kihei

1. Our ancestors traveled far
      to find this paradise by guiding star
   Now it's time to seek for ourselves
   Elusive answers that books on shelves
      do not reveal
   Now it's time to take to the road
   The lack of movement makes our dreams corrode
      hope is gained through ordeal

   But where does the road lead to
   Where are you when we most need you
      brother George, our helmsman in the night
   The sea has taken you as its own
   Now I'm feeling more and more alone
      as I stare at the water seeking a guiding light

2. Yes, we all have journeyed far
      looking for that same guiding star
   I saw the writing on the wall
   And I took it for a child's scrawl
      just graffiti
   I watched the double hulled canoe
   Sail till it disappeared from view
      toward Tahiti

   But where does the voyage lead to
   Where are you, Eddie, when we most need you
      I'm not sure but the stars seem to give a clue
   I see the starlight in children's eyes
   And at once I can make the ties
      you lit our hearts so we can carry it through

3. Peace is an elusive kind of friend
      Island living is conducive towards this end

But I learned that the real chase
Only starts when you find your pace
    some peace of mind
Through the efforts of a dying race
May we find our rightful place
    in the nick of time

Where does this song lead to
Brother George, help me through
    brother Kimo, what more can I sing
In a way we're all lost at sea
Trying to find that harmony
    guided by the sacrifices of you three
Searching for the right key
Seeking some harmony

Dr. Emmett Aluli.

Alexis Higdon

In the Spirit of George and Kimo

Noa Emmett Aluli, M.D.
The Protect Kaho'olawe 'Ohana
Hui Ala Loa

Na 'olua e ka'ika'i mai ia makou i kou kakou hana kupono o ka 'aina. By you two are we led in our upright work for the sake of the land.

Ke ha'upu mai nei ka hali'a aloha. The cherished memories remain.

Keoki a me Kimo. E ho'omaika'i makou ia 'olua. Ko makou hoa i ha'awi lilo ai i ke ola no ka pono ame ka ho'omau 'ana o ka lahui Hawai'i a me ke ea o ka 'aina. We salute you as brothers, George Helm and Kimo Mitchell, brothers whom we have known; who have given your lives in the struggle to preserve and perpetuate the native Hawaiian culture, and the life of the land.

This is our living tribute—to continue your unfinished work.

Eight years ago, we were *'opio* in our actions against the many injustices to the Hawaiian that moved George and Kimo to act. Now we are the *makua* of the *aloha 'aina* movement; and soon we will become *kupuna* as we continue to grow in our ability and commitment to living our traditions as native practitioners. The presence of George and Kimo is still felt in our daily activities, whether on Kaho'olawe, Moloka'i, or Ke'anae to Kipahulu on Maui. Their respective visions have added stability and credibility to our approaches. George was a brother to whom we looked for leadership and vision. Kimo was a brother whom we turned to for support, a brother who was always there when help was needed. Our relationships with them have given us the spirit of *'ohana* to endure all the political and economic complexities of returning to the *'aina,* so that the *kamali'i* have a better opportunity to persevere in sustaining the subsistence Hawaiian culture and religion of these lands.

Keoni Fairbanks and Keli'i "Skippy" Ioane, helping to build a traditional hale *at Hakioawa Bay on Kahoolawe. The hale symbolizes the resettlement efforts of the PKO.*

Ed Greevy

On Kaho'olawe, our civil suit against the Navy has resulted in the re-discovery of over 2000 archaeological sites and features, and *mauka-makai* settlement areas throughout the entire island. Kaho'olawe is now recognized on the National Register of Historic Places as a Historic District because of its cultural significance and scientific value to Hawaii's people.

A Consent Decree agreement in partial settlement of our suit over the use of Kaho'olawe, has been signed with the Navy assuring our access to the island, complete eradication of goats, soil conservation and erosion control, protection of archaeological sites, and clearance of surface explosive ordnance. The Protect Kaho'olawe 'Ohana is recognized as the stewards of the *moku 'aina* Kaho'olawe.

We still go to Kaho'olawe to strengthen our relationship with the land, and to initiate revegetation projects in order to re-establish the native environment and *re-green* Kaho'olawe. There we are building a traditional Hawaiian *hale* to symbolize our re-settlement of the island. In this regard, we pay respect to the ancient spirit of the land. At *Makahiki* time we honor the god Lono and his Lonoikamakahiki forms for the nurturance of the island. Through our actions, including our maneuvering of legal and bureaucratic policies, we will firmly establish Kaho'olawe as a cultural resource for Hawaiian people, a *pu'uhonua* for generations to come.

On Maui, the *Hana District Pohaku* was formed by those close to and inspired by George and Kimo, and has become the example for native Hawaiian community corporations making practical use of traditional and appropriate technology for crop farming such as *kalo* cultivation and fishing. In addition, the group has organized successfully to research genealogy, plan for the use of lands in Kipahulu, fight court cases against adverse possession of kuleana lands and to protect water access rights.

On Moloka'i, *Hui Alaloa* continues to struggle to guarantee alternative and traditional land uses. This includes the right of access to the mountains and beaches.

One of many petroglyphs found by PKO members.

Ed Greevy

On Hawai'i, Hawaiian Home Lands issues are the focus of much of our organizing. From the time of the Hilo Airport protest in 1978 to the present Kaulana Case—whether or not to build a boat ramp in Ka'u—much of the land rights researched by George have been coming to settlement.

And on Kaua'i and O'ahu, many of the land use issues revolve around Hawaiians who believe in and practice the *aloha 'aina* tradition established by George, a tradition that Kimo's Ke'anae roots fostered. *Save Nukoli'i* on Kaua'i and *Aloha 'Aina Na Opio* on the Waianae Coast of O'ahu are examples of groups involved in the fight for traditional land rights.

The lives of George and Kimo have inspired many to advocate greater self-determination for Hawaiians through access and use rights of alienated lands on every island.

We acknowledge and are thankful for the connections made by George and Kimo to our cultural past. We are thankful to other brothers, sisters, and kupuna, who attracted by George and Kimo, have travelled the islands with us, and given us direction and confidence to "Stop the Bombing" and return Kaho'olawe to Hawaiian control. Our continuing efforts at organizing and networking here in our local communities and across the Pacific are dedicated in large part to George and Kimo. We will always remember them with aloha.

E ho'omau e ho'omahuamahua ke aloha o ka 'aina. The love for the land shall persist and it shall grow.

One of Kahoolawe's beautiful sand beaches.

Ed Greevy

Ed Greevy

'Ohana members at Hakioawa enjoying a respite from the task of greening *Kahoolawe.*

Heading toward Kahoolawe.

Ed Greevy

Huaka'i

Joseph Balaz

Make strong the cord
which binds the canoe,
we are sailing home.

The storm
which swamped
our peaceful voyage
is behind us now.

The wind lashed,
the waves pounded,
but we did not go down.

Make strong the cord
which binds the canoe,
we are sailing home.

Kahoolawe Remembers

Wayne Muromoto

Aloha no—

Notes on Contributors

NOA EMMETT ALULI is a General-Family physician on Molokai. He is a founding member of Hui Alaloa and the Protect Kahoolawe Ohana. He has also helped organize many Native Hawaiian groups throughout the Hawaiian Islands.

JOSEPH P. BALAZ is the editor of *Ramrod.* His poetry has been published in *Seaweeds and Constructions, Mana, Hapa,* and *Bamboo Ridge.* He works in Laie and lives in Punaluu.

MALANI BILYEU is an original member of Kalapana. He is currently working on his second solo album which will feature the single, "Ballad of George Helm."

DON CHAPMAN is the *Honolulu Advertiser's* three-dot columnist.

ERIC CHOCK is a local poet.

RICHARD HAMASAKI's concrete poem and MARK HAMASAKI's serigraph, "Death at Sea," is one of a series of twelve silkscreens on permanent display at the Basel Youth Hostel in Switzerland.

ALVIN ISAACS is "79 years young." He has written hundreds of songs, some of which were sung by George Helm.

IMAIKALANI KALAHELE is a Hawaiian artist.

KALANI MEINECKE hopes someday to make a meaningful contribution to that which is Hawaiian. He is meanwhile a researcher and an assistant professor of Hawaiian at the University of Hawaii at Manoa.

HARRY K. MITCHELL, SR., is the father of Kimo Mitchell. He still grows taro in Keanae. He is, in his own words, "still taking care of nature... I goin' die with nature, just like my kupuna."

RODNEY MORALES lives in Honolulu with his wife, Ann, and their contribution to the class of 2001, Dan-Michael.

WAYNE MUROMOTO was raised in Waialua, Oahu. He began drawing as a kid on paper, his parents' old Dodge, in the dirt, and on the walls of the house. His parents repainted the walls, bought a new car, and put asphalt on the dirt. He

View from Moaulaiki, the highest point of Kahoolawe.

Ed Greevy

still draws on paper. His art has been in numerous local art shows, publications, and public and private collections.

JON OSORIO and RANDY BORDEN perform as the duo Jon and Randy. They have recorded two albums. Their album, *Hawaiian Eyes,* features the song "Hawaiian Soul."

'ILIMA PI'IANAI'A was a friend of George Helm's.

WALTER RITTE, JR. is a trustee of the Office of Hawaiian Affairs from the island of Molokai. Currently he is working on a long-range project to restore the *ahapua'a* concept of mauka-makai land divisions.

FORTUNATO TEHO is Hawaii's only national award winning horticultural journalist.

WAYNE WESTLAKE (1947-1984) was born on Maui. His works have been published locally in Honolulu, nationally across the mainland, internationally in Argentina, Australia, Canada, England, Fiji, India, and Japan. The *Kahoolawe Chants, Legends, Poems, Stories by Children of Maui* was first produced in mimeo and self-published by Wayne in 1977.